Anti-Harassment Training Does Not Work

Transformative Learning:
Moving Information
from Head to Heart

DR. CANDY KHAN

Anti-Harassment Training Does Not Work

https://www.facebook.com/candy.khan.71
https://www.instagram.com/candykhan1545/?hl=en
https://www.linkedin.com/in/dr-candy-khan-43101518/

Pensiero Press

www.PensieroPress.com

All rights reserved. No part of this book may be reproduced or transmitted in any form or by any means, graphic, electronic or mechanical, including photocopying, recording, taping, Web distribution, or by any informational storage and retrieval system without written permission from the publisher except for the inclusion of brief quotations in a review or scholarly reference.

Books are available through Pensiero Press at special discounts for bulk purchases for the purpose of sales promotion, seminar attendance, or educational purposes. Special volumes can be created for specific purposes and to organizational specifications. Please contact us for further details.

Individual authors own the copyright to their individual materials. Pensiero Press has each author's permission to reprint.

Copyright © 2022 by Pensiero Press

Volume ISBN: 978-1-7376538-5-1

*Kindle and electronic versions available

Cover and interior: Gary Rosenberg • www.thebookcouple.com

10 9 8 7 6 5 4 3 2 1

CONTENTS

Testimonials vii
Foreword xi
Acknowledgments xvii
Preface xix

Introduction 1
Chapter One. Social, Cultural and Political Context 5
Chapter Two. Workplace Harassment 11
Chapter Three. Workplace Learning 29
Chapter Four. Social Location, Positionality,
    and Intersectionality 41
Chapter Five. Transformative Learning and
    Anti-Harassment Training 47
Chapter Six. Whole Person Learning Approach 59
Conclusion 73

Appendix 75
Final Word 85
Bibliography 91
About the Author 101
Coming Soon 102

This book is dedicated to all the workers experiencing harassment and the policy makers, practitioners, educators, and facilitators working toward eradicating workplace harassment.

TESTIMONIALS

Pauline Melnyk

I am fortunate to have crossed paths with Dr. Candy Khan in 2014, our paths have intersected at crucial points in both our careers. I am very grateful for the opportunity to endorse *Anti-Harassment Training Does Not Work*. It is a book personalized in practical advice for the facilitator and educator in today's modern workplace.

Stop and imagine your reality changed, perhaps challenged, whether you are in a formal or informal leadership position, this is a read for you to engage. It doesn't matter the extent of the teaching or training, the intent of the process intervention of change is a crucial role of the facilitator or intervenor. Training gives us a language to communicate. Courage gives us a voice to what we have learned, experienced or expressed. Dr. Khan challenges us to remain hopeful, regain a sense of self, of healing, of overcoming trauma in our lives and more importantly our workplaces.

This thing called work should not repeat previous patterns year-after-year. The whole-person comes to work not just the part of them that you want. Be prepared to accept authentically and genuinely the whole person not the knowledge worker, labourer, care giver, health provider, physician etc. Your workforce is the heart, soul, practice and experience for the organization to succeed. Embrace the embodied sense of work and learning, engage coaches and mentors to transition the collective experience of psychological and sociological safety. Do the work, truly listen to others, reduce judgments, and increase authentic communication with compassion and heart.

With gratitude.

—PAULINE MELNYK CMP CPHR PCC WFA; Accredited Trainer & Consultant, Professional Certified Coach; Innovative Practitioner of Regenerative Leadership and Workplace Restoration, Melnyk Consultancy Ltd • www.melnykconsultancy.com

Fahad Mughal

It is my honor to endorse *Anti-Harassment Training Does Not Work—Transformative Learning: Moving the Information from the Head to Heart*. I am glad that we finally have literature on this subject backed by research and study. Dr. Candy Khan, who has been a great influence in my life as a friend and a mentor, has inspired me by her academic work and her extraordinary communication style. I congratulate Candy on yet another achievement on authoring this masterpiece, which in my opinion is going to be transformative in organizational 'anti-harassment' training programs.

FAHAD MUGHAL is a business consultant specializing in process improvement and reforming public policy. An alumnus of Harvard and Oxford University, Fahad is also a passionate filmmaker committed to make films on social justice. He is the writer, director, and producer of the film *Overqualified*, which focuses on life and struggles of internationally trained professionals in the Canadian job market.

Testimonials

Linda Sahli

Anti-Harassment Training Does Not Work—Transformative Learning: Moving the Information from the Head to Heart by Dr. Candy Khan is an essential resource for organizations and leaders who truly want to see transformative change in themselves, their colleagues and the systems they are responsible for leading. Dr. Khan offers a compelling case for why current anti-harassment training programs are often unsuccessful and follows that with a compelling case for why. Most importantly, Dr. Khan provides readers with practical advice regarding how to build a transformative learning environment that will allow for true change. Thank you, Dr. Khan, for doing and sharing this important work.

—Linda Sahli, BA, Juris Doctor,
Non-Profit Executive Leader

Harriet Tinka

The book is thorough and specific and aims to educate employees and employers. It is a complete guide to understanding and preventing harassment in the workplace.
The author outlines the historical and social context of harassment, and I was left in awe at the shared relatable stories. Having the lived experience and taken anti-harassment training, it is clear to me why anti-harassment training alone is not transformative. The written style is conversational and easy to follow. It is a long-awaited book.

—HARRIET TINKA, BBA, CPA, CMA, CCP, DTM;
EmpoweredMe Inc Founder/CEO • www.empoweredme.ca

FOREWORD

Denise Koster, B.A.A., P.H.Ec. CTM PI

In our work lives, we are intertwined with peers, subordinates, and supervisors of different genders, sexual orientations, ethnicities, ages, and religious backgrounds. To think that there will never be conflict is naive.

Over the past 35 years, working in the capacity of a unionized employee, middle manager, clinical director, and licensed private investigator, I have learned many valuable lessons. The most important lesson is the critical need for organizations to have effective and responsive leaders to guide their employees down the road to success. Employee satisfaction is critical and ultimately results in the retention of creative and dedicated personnel proud to work alongside senior leadership to meet the organization's mission, vision, and values to create a respectful, responsive, and sought-after employer of choice.

Over my career, I have encountered many organizations that claim to have a *zero-tolerance* policy on workplace harassment and violence, but that is not true. Harassing behaviours, regardless of the organizational positions, are tolerated every day. A more realistic approach is establishing codes of conduct and comprehensive transformational strategies for dealing with conflicts that build trust and allow employees to feel safe.

Anti-Harassment Training Does Not Work

Leaders need to be aware of the key drivers behind conflicts in the workplace to effectively address them before serious problems arise. Data from the 2016 General Social Survey on Canadians at Work and Home (GSS) focused on workplace harassment experienced by respondents aged 15 to 64 and who worked for pay at some point in the past year. Workplace harassment includes verbal abuse, humiliating behaviour, threats to persons, physical violence, and unwanted sexual attention or sexual harassment. A summary of the findings indicates:

- 19% of women and 13% of men reported that they had experienced harassment in their workplace in the past year; the most common type of workplace harassment was verbal abuse, followed by humiliating behaviour and threats.

- Women were more likely to report sexual harassment in their workplace (4%) than men (less than 1%).

- 47% of men and 34% of women whom a supervisor or manager had harassed had a weak sense of belonging to their current organization, compared with 16% of both women and men, who said they had not been harassed at work in the past year.

Most recently, in the 2020 Statistics Canada report by Marta Burczycka, "Workers' experiences of inappropriate sexualized behaviours, sexual assault and gender-based discrimination in Canadian provinces,' highlighted that 47% of workers either witnessed or experienced some form of inappropriate sexualized or discriminatory behaviour. Ten percent of females had experienced workplace discrimination based on gender compared to 4% of males. For 44% of women and 36% of men in cases where the targeting of discrimination was based on gender, gender identity, or sexual orientation, a person in a position of authority was identified as the perpetrator of the behaviour. The report further identified that discrimination and other inappropriate sexualized or gender-based discrimination occurred most often among LGBTQ2 people, young people, and people with disabilities.

I know from first-hand experience the devastating consequences of workplace harassment, both for individuals and the organizations that employ them. Trust, morale, communication, teamwork, and quality of service are all derailed. There are significant costs associated with what I see as an epidemic, including productivity drops, sick leave, staff turnover, and lawsuits. The prevention of workplace harassment and ultimately, litigation cost and liability of an organization lies within the powers of effective leadership. Given the far-reaching and harmful effects of workplace harassment—for targets, bystanders, and organizations—employers must foster collaborative workplace cultures where harassment is taboo and eradicated before it takes root.

Research shows that harassed and bullied employees frequently develop mental health problems, costing employers $20 billion a year. According to *The Canadian Business Journal*, Dr. Warren Shepell, a pioneer in Employee Assistance Programs (EAPs), harassed and bullied employees frequently develop mental health problems — the employee becomes fearful of the workplace and the organization suffers through the employee's lowered productivity, absenteeism, and disability — translating into thousands of dollars. Canada's Mental Health Commission estimates that coping with mental health issues costs the Canadian economy $51 billion, with $20 billion directly attributable to workplace stresses.

In addition to the direct financial impact of mental health issues, there are also costs associated with mental-health complications arising from dealing with physical injury, recruiting, or training replacement workers, and the effect on both the mental and physical health of co-workers who have to handle an increased workload, reports OHS Canada magazine. According to the TIME'S UP Foundation and the Institute for Women's Policy Research's most recent report:

1. Costs of sexual harassment can include job loss and unemployment, lower earnings, missed opportunities for advancement, forced job changes, and loss of critical employer-sponsored benefits like health insurance and pension contributions.

2. Factors like immigration status, lack of funds, or lack of information about worker rights keep individuals from seeking legal advice. Failure to act and retaliation by those in positions of power—such as supervisors, human resources, and colleagues—magnify the costs and impact of harassment.

Beyond the adverse mental health impacts, new research shows that bullying might also seriously affect physical health. Researchers at the University of Copenhagen found that the incidence of heart-related problems (heart disease or stroke) increased by 59% in those bullied compared with those who were not bullied. In November of 2013, Eric Donovan from the province of Prince Edward Island suffered a cardiac arrest brought on by workplace stress. Eric's wife was awarded benefits after his death was attributed to ongoing bullying at the group home where he worked.

Bullying in the workplace can also devastate bystanders who witness inappropriate behaviour. Researchers from Sheffield University's Institute of Work Psychology found that even without experiencing direct bullying, staff who observed the behaviour experienced declines in their work-related wellbeing, including feeling more depressed. Earlier research by Singapore Management University similarly concluded that the vicarious experience of incivility at work affects the mental health of bystanders, which in turn affects their physical health.

A recent survey by the UK's Chartered Institute of Personnel and Development showed that almost one-quarter of employees believe bullying and harassment are swept under the rug in their company. Organizations have a legal obligation to protect employees from harassment and bullying. Failing to do so can have significant consequences. In recent years, there has been a dramatic increase in damage awards. An Ontario court awarded $100,000 in damages for intentional infliction of mental suffering against a manager and $150,000 in aggravated damages against the employer.

Although all workplaces must comply with anti-harassment and discrimination laws, in the GGS findings, 32% of women and 26% of men said that their employer had not provided them with information on reporting sexual harassment and sexual assault. The majority of employee-driven discrimination and harassment situations are preventable but mitigating the inevitable conflicts requires a holistic response — from both management and staff. As thoroughly examined by Dr. Khan's research, implementing solid policies and incorporating transformative annual training opportunities around workplace harassment and complaint resolution and creating an environment where people feel empowered to speak out are vital to designing workplaces that foster dignity and respect. Without a robust framework, many employees will leave the organization and potentially file an external health and safety or human rights complaint due to the organization's failure to provide a psychologically safe workplace, thereby subjecting the organization to limitless human and legal costs. As Dr. Khan summarizes in her book, *Anti-Harassment Training Does Not Work* "anti-harassment training is only one step, albeit an important one, to transformative change in an organization."

ACKNOWLEDGMENTS

First and foremost, I want to thank my family: Roger, Omar, Lyila, Dalida, and Faisal for their unconditional love and support. My granddaughter Zahra, who brings me down to earth in seconds by reminding me that we are born with a blank slate but acquire biases along the way. My brother Shaz for always pushing me to pursue my dreams and being there for me during the dark times. You are my rock! I have learned so much from your experience of being bullied and harassed, yet you persevered and remained calm.

I want to thank my good friends Pauline Melynk, Cara Robertson, and Denise Young for listening to me and being reliable allies. Thank you, Marnie Ferguson, for all the edits and helping me with the structure and converting my dissertation into a readable book that is accessible to a layperson.

Deep gratitude to Cheryl Lentz for believing in me and guiding me throughout the publishing process.

Last, but not the least, Denise Koster, who has been my source of inspiration and continuous learning. I learn so much from you every day. You are a brilliant investigator and the only one who truly understands the intricacies of workplace harassment and the importance of an effective anti-harassment program design.

PREFACE

I worked as a senior diversity and inclusion consultant for a local government in a mid-western Canadian city. One of my duties was developing a curriculum for anti-harassment training. *Harassment* refers to any form of verbal, visual, or physical conduct that could create or contribute to an intimidating, offensive, or hostile working environment (Alberta Human Rights, 2019; Bison-Rapp, 2018; Einerson et al., 2010). Anti-harassment training is an opportunity to communicate and reinforce an organization's anti-harassment policy and explain the complaint process and reporting options. The intent of anti-harassment training is to discourage and possibly eliminate workplace harassment. I designed the anti-harassment curriculum, rolled out the training plan, hired external facilitators, and led the workshops in which over 6000 staff participated. However, despite continuous training, the harassment complaints continued to rise, which led me to think about the design of the training itself.

In 2010, one of my close acquaintances was presenting an academic paper for her doctoral program at the university in the same department where I had studied and graduated. I decided to attend the seminar to support my friend and to reconnect with my previous supervisors. One of the professors I knew and had worked with as a research assistant expressed her pleasure in seeing me. Another professor who had been my supervisor on a project suggested that I should consider coming back to the department and completing a Ph.D. degree. He suggested that the department could benefit from my lived experience, in particular the practical experience working at the local government.

I was thrilled to hear my previous professors thought that I was capable of completing a Ph.D. and teaching at the university level and my supervisor at work supported my decision to return to university to complete my graduate degree. One of the professors asked me a poignant question: *What keeps you up at night?* I told her I was concerned that traditional training approaches in anti-harassment training such as a lecture and a PowerPoint presentation were not shifting attitudes and behaviours. Organizations consider *bums in the chair* as success. In other words, organizations measure training effectiveness by the number of people trained. While research suggests that anti-harassment training will likely increase the number of complaints, I wanted to explore an alternative teaching method that could potentially reduce workplace harassment, but I did not know what that methodology was at that time. The professor supported the idea, agreed to supervise my work, and consequently I applied for the graduate program in 2011.

Unfortunately, 3 months after I started the Ph.D. program, my supervisor could no longer provide academic support due to health challenges and she referred me to another professor who specialized in adult and workplace learning. My first supervisor sadly passed away in 2015 and I started working with her colleague informally. Shortly thereafter, our department went through massive changes, a new dean, chair, and several professors, including my supervisor, resigned and I started working with a third professor. From him, I discovered the concept of embodiment. Embodiment may be physical, cognitive, or emotional, and refers to the processes whereby a person's life experiences are literally incorporated into their body. It can also mean being in touch with the physical sensations in the body, and being in our bodies, consciously or unconsciously.

My new advisor encouraged me to read academic and non-academic books and articles on the sociology of the body and that formed a solid foundation to understand the role of the body. However, he was a political theorist and consequently steered me toward political theories, including structures, agencies, and capitalism. His perspective was different than mine and though I agreed with his ideas wholeheartedly, I felt that his approach in interrogating workplace harassment was beyond the scope of my studies. Regardless, I read numerous books and articles, and shaped the chapters to appease my supervisor.

After spending 9 months drafting the candidacy proposal, the supervisory committee did not meet with me prior to the candidacy exam so I did not know if I was on the right path. One committee member I approached just before the exam told me that she did not think that I was on the right path but was reluctant to guide me because she was not comfortable challenging my supervisor.

Suffice it to say that I passed the candidacy exam but had to do major revisions. Ultimately, I rewrote the entire document, severed my relationship with my supervisor, and went searching for another one. The new supervisor specialized in environmental and global studies. She rejected all previous writing; hence, I authored the dissertation for the third time. This time I relied on literature on metaphysics and Eastern tradition and religious studies that focused on the role of the body. Unfortunately, we could not agree on the style of writing in the thesis, and I re-wrote the entire thesis for the fourth time. It was not until 2 years later that I landed with a supervisor and committee that supported my view that it was important to view the human being as a whole person in the context of learning.

While the committee valued head knowledge, they also valued self-awareness, emotional growth, social growth, and spiritual development. Fortunately, I was able to complete my studies and I defended my dissertation in 2021.

It is important for me to showcase the history of my doctorate journey for the reader to appreciate where I started and where I ended up. There was so much more that I wanted to say while writing the dissertation over the course of 9 years but was unable to because the supervisors could not relate to my work; after all, there were footprints of 11 different advisors with distinct philosophies and styles.

Thus, I wanted to write a book about anti-harassment training in the workplace that incorporated my dissertation, lived experiences, and personal voice. I wanted to write a book that was accessible in terms of language and suitable for a variety of educators and practitioners. The main point I want to make is that the learners/workers learn in different ways; they are not a cognition (mind) on a stick. Humans have a body, mind, emotions, and spirit. Hence, mind and body cannot be separated, and we all learn differently. Some learners rely on rational thinking and reasoning, what I shall refer as *head learning*. Other learners rely on embodiment, body knowledge, and sensations in the body to make sense of their experience. Head learning (the PowerPoint and lecture) alone might be ineffective in moving the information from the head to the heart when it comes to the topic of workplace harassment. It is time that practitioners consider a holistic approach in teaching an anti-harassment workshop. A holistic perspective in teaching an anti-harassment training means acknowledging the body, mind, emotions, and spirit are present and impact learning.

INTRODUCTION

Workplace anti-harassment training is not a panacea, but it has the potential to reduce workplace harassment. There are several pieces to the puzzle. For instance, an organization needs a robust anti-harassment policy, leadership that models respectful workplace behaviours, and sanctions for individuals who violate the anti-harassment policy irrespective of their position. Currently, training is mandatory in most mid- and large-sized organizations across Canada, therefore current teaching approaches must be interrogated, and alternative methods need to be explored. Organizations should be able to offer an effective anti-harassment training that has an impact; thereby reducing incidents of workplace harassment and making workers feel safe.

Anti-harassment training is only one step, albeit an important one, to transformative change in an organization. There are many factors that lead to workplace harassment including organizational structure (hierarchical, collaborative, and network), leadership styles, reward systems, and workplace culture, to name a few. At the same time, anti-harassment training is ubiquitous across North America, and it does not appear to be subsiding. Considering organizations are investing money, time, and effort in providing training, it is worth exploring anti-harassment training design.

Anti-Harassment Training Does Not Work

What follows is an overview of the social and cultural climate of the times that provides a backdrop to any discussion of anti-harassment training. This is followed by a discussion of workplace harassment, including an examination of sexual harassment, a common problem in many workplaces, and at which training is particularly focused, and how anti-harassment training is situated.

The next part of the book includes discussion of learning and training in the workplace, followed by the important issue of social location and the lens through which a participant experiences anti-harassment training in the workplace. Social location is a combination of many factors including their age, gender, culture, race, and other aspects of their personality and experience that will influence how they interact with others and how they view their workplaces and their co-workers and colleagues.

Transformative learning and how it can impact the way in which training is delivered is explained, followed by a discussion of the whole person learning approach, and what came from a study that examined the experiences of participants attending mandatory anti-harassment training in a hierarchical, bureaucratic, and unionized workplace located in western Canada. The purpose of the study was to explore trainees' perceptions of the mandatory, anti-harassment training and to determine whether a transformative learning approach, specifically a whole person learning approach to anti-harassment training design, might provide a more effective teaching approach for anti-harassment training.

There were six participants in the study with direct experience in attending a one-time, in-person, 3 hour mandatory, company-sponsored anti-harassment training. I explored the whole person teaching approach to anti-harassment training. The whole person incorporates cognitive (rational) thinking and embodiment (feelings, emotions, and spirit).

The participants felt the anti-harassment training was a closed and mechanical process. This is to say that training was mostly *head learning* and did not engage the body, emotions, and spirit. Based on findings from the study, anti-harassment training curriculum should engage the whole person learning involving experiential, emotive, spiritual, and embodied learning. Training has to be transformative, potentially moving the information from the head to the heart and may offer a more effective teaching approach.

There has been no similar study in North America that explores anti-harassment training though a transformative and embodied lens.

CHAPTER ONE
SOCIAL, CULTURAL, AND POLITICAL CONTEXT

There is a lack of research regarding effectiveness of anti-harassment training, and in particular, research that includes participants' perceptions of such training. Therefore, my research proved to be timely because there have been several recent high-profile cases (Weinsten, Epstein, Crosby, Ghomeshi, and Nygard) of workplace harassment that have propelled a strong desire for training to address the problem of workplace harassment. In addition, there is a statute of limitation on workplace harassment in Canada because complaints must be made within 1 year of the alleged incident, which adds to the importance of anti-harassment training design.

This chapter looks at the social, cultural, and political climate that provided a backdrop to my research into anti-harassment training. Two major developments pertinent to the topic gained international attention: the rise of the #Me Too Movement and the response by the Starbucks' Chief Executive Officer (CEO) to an incident of racial harassment in one the company's American stores. These two cases originated in the

United States, yet they arguably had an impact on the discussion of sexual and racial harassment in Canada. In Canada, there were also signs that tolerance of harassment in the workplace was at a crossroads and two high profile cases of sexual assault came before the courts involving Peter Nygard, a clothing designer and manufacturer charged with sexual assault and CBC radio personality Jian Ghomeshi facing similar charges.

#Me Too Movement

Tarana Burke, an African American civil rights activist, started using the phrase *Me Too* to raise awareness of the pervasiveness of sexual abuse and assault against women of colour in the United States. The #MeToo movement (#MeToo) is a visible empowerment act rooted in empathy that lets survivors know they are not alone in their journeys. Though Burke's campaign initially supported women of colour, the #MeToo movement ultimately developed into a global action that heightened awareness of bullying, harassment, and sexual abuse. The #MeToo movement took place alongside or in tandem with the controversy starting in 2017 surrounding Hollywood film producer Harvey Weinstein, who faced six allegations of workplace sexual harassment and unwanted physical contact.

The allegations led to a burgeoning number of complaints by dozens of women who came forward accusing Weinstein and other famous Hollywood men of sexual assault and misconduct, which popularized the phrase the Weinstein Ripple Effect. Since 2018, the guilty finding in the sexual assault case against Bill Cosby has been celebrated as a major win for the #MeToo movement. Along with the Weinstein Ripple Effect, the verdict against Cosby demonstrated a shift in North American and Western societies from doubting the victims to believing their accounts of sexual abuse, a shift that has had significant ramifications for the justice system. Nonetheless, although the #MeToo movement has allegedly removed the burden of shame that often prevents women and men from coming forward with allegations of sexual harassment, many workers may continue to be inhibited from bringing forward concerns about deviant workplace behaviours, such as general workplace harassment and sexual harassment. Some may be afraid of negative employment consequences; others have experienced previous unsatisfactory experiences when they voiced their concerns in the past, and there are those who did not report any incidents because of a lack of action by the organization. Organizations where the alleged sexual harassment occurred are often cited to have a policy against sexual harassment and many claim to offer anti-harassment training.

The Starbucks' Initiative

In May 2018, two African American men were wrongfully accused of trespassing and then arrested at a Starbucks coffee retail outlet in Philadelphia. The incident began when the two men were accused of wanting to use the public restroom, but the barista informed the men that the washroom was strictly for paying customers. The two men refused to leave. The barista then called the police. The African American men stated that they were waiting for a third party to arrive, hence, the reason for not ordering items. In the meantime, police handcuffed and arrested the two men for trespassing. The CEO of Starbucks, Kevin Johnson, reacted to the news immediately and promised to revamp the organization's management training program to include unconscious bias training to address the discriminatory act of racial profiling. Johnson said its American company-owned stores and corporate offices would be closed on the afternoon of May 29, 2018, for the training.

The Starbucks' training initiative compelled the closure of more than 8,000 stores in the United States for several hours. The closures cost the company approximately $21.5 million Canadian dollars in lost sales, according to Bloomberg's calculations (Fletcher, 2018). It is notable that this training involved 175,000 employees. Employees who attended the 4-hour training experienced mixed results. Many took to the media and wrote their narratives. Some suggested that the training was well done; others stated that training was blanketed to every store, instead of being tailored to different demographics; training focused exclusively on Black Americans.

Rideau Hall, RCMP, and Canadian Armed Forces

There were several cases of bullying, harassment, sexual harassment, and discrimination at all levels of the government in Canada. In 2020, allegations came to light that the Governor General of Canada, Julie Payette, had created a toxic climate of harassment and verbal abuse at Rideau Hall. In 2020, the Canadian federal government published new regulations to prevent harassment and violence in federal workplaces. Ironically, the government moved to offer anti-harassment training to all staff, but there is no data made public whether the training is effective in reducing incidents of harassment.

For decades, the Royal Canadian Mounted Police (RCMP) struggled with the problem of workplace harassment, bullying, intimidation, and sexual harassment. In June 2020, the RCMP launched an independent centre for harassment resolution. The Canadian armed forces continue to struggle with mitigating workplace harassment, in particular sexual harassment. The armed forces explored new training and educational materials with hopes of mitigating sexual misconduct. The examples noted above highlight that bullying, harassment, and sexual harassment are not new phenomena; the high-profile cases are part of public discourse, thereby necessitating an effective anti-harassment policy and company-sponsored anti-harassment program that is effective.

High-Profile Sexual Assault Cases

Two other cases reflect prominence of sexual assault charges against high-profile individuals who lend credence to the need for an examination of workplace anti-harassment training.

In 2015, three young women accused radio host Gian Ghomeshi, all about 20 years his junior, claiming that Ghomeshi was physically violent toward them without their consent during sexual encounters. After being charged with one count of choking and four counts of sexual assault, Ghomeshi claimed that his ex-girlfriends spread lies about him and orchestrated a campaign with other women to smear him. One woman who worked with him at the Canadian Broadcasting Corporation (CBC) talked about being sexually assaulted and reporting the incident to the producers of the show; however, the producers did not take any action. In 2016, Ghomeshi was acquitted of all charges.

In 2020, Peter Nygard a former designer, who ran an international fashion business from Winnipeg, Canada, was charged with six counts of sexual assault and forcible confinement, sex trafficking, and racketeering conspiracy. Allegations dated back to when Nygard was in his twenties. In 1980, Nygard was charged with rape; however, the woman refused to testify. There was a class action lawsuit that dates back to 1977. None of the allegations have been proven in court and Nygard maintains his innocence.

CHAPTER TWO
WORKPLACE HARASSMENT

Workplace harassment is a broad term and is studied under different names, including sexual harassment, racial harassment, and bullying. Workplace harassment alludes to belittling or threatening behaviours directed at an individual worker or a group of workers. Sexual harassment is any unwelcome sexual behaviour that adversely affects or threatens to affect, directly or indirectly, a person's job security, working conditions, or prospects for promotion or earnings; or prevents a person from getting a job. Bullying is usually seen as acts or verbal comments that could mentally hurt or isolate a person in the workplace. Harassment is an umbrella term that spills over into racial harassment and discrimination. In my expertise, I define racial harassment is when a person expresses hostility against or brings into contempt or ridicules another person on the grounds of their colour, race, ethnic, or national origins. Racial harassment is hurtful, offensive, and has a detrimental effect on that person's employment, job performance, and satisfaction.

I focus exclusively on workplace harassment and conceptualize harassment as behaviours that are unwelcome to the recipient, found to be offensive and demeaning, and would be considered by a reasonable person to create an intimidating, hostile, or offensive environment at work.

Workplace harassment has a negative impact at an individual and organizational level. At the individual level, an employee who is the target of workplace harassment may experience a variety of psychological and physical effects, which may include the onset of stress-related disorders such as: loss of sleep, loss of appetite, inability to concentrate, and a reduction in productivity both at home and at work. The implications of workplace harassment on the organizational level can be equally devastating. From an employer's perspective, the presence of such influences in the workplace can result in decreased employee morale, which in turn may breed increased levels of absenteeism, higher turnover rates, losses in overall productivity, and ultimately damage the organization's reputation. Hence today, employers are legally responsible for creating a workplace free from harassment and discrimination.

Tracking Workplace Harassment in Canada

Various organizations in Canada collect data on workplace harassment for different purposes. For example, data on workplace harassment is collected to gauge workplace culture and mitigate risks. Data was collected for this purpose in 2017, when the Canadian Federal Government surveyed labour organizations, employer organizations, federal government departments and agencies, academics, and advocacy groups, and found that 60% of Canadian workers in the federal government experienced workplace harassment. The Canadian Human Rights Commission (CHRC) tracks human rights complaints for federally regulated employees. Provincial governments legislate standards. For example, Alberta Occupational Health and Safety (AOHS) mandates that all non-government employers provide a safe and healthful workplace for their employees; consequently, AOHS tracks harassment complaints. The Alberta Human Rights Commission (AHRC) tracks human rights complaints for human rights code for government and non-government employees. While provincial and federal departments collect data on workplace harassment, there is no single entity that aggregates the data at a national level in Canada.

What is Anti-Harassment Training?

Anti-harassment training is generally rooted in the corporate anti-harassment policy and is a collaboration between administration, unions, and management association. The policy highlights definitions of personal harassment, sexual harassment, and discrimination. The purpose of anti-harassment training is to educate employees about what constitutes rude, uncivil, and disrespectful behaviour such as bullying, harassment, and discrimination. Training highlights the detrimental impact of disrespectful behaviour, and ways to resolve workplace conflicts. It is also used to inform employees about company policies and human rights' legislation. In my experience, employers offer anti-harassment training mainly to comply with government regulations. Organizations thereby insulate themselves against legal action by asserting that they have trained their employees; hence, the company is absolved from responsibility should such legal actions occur. It is not surprising that many employees react with indifference and even cynicism to the training requirements in their workplaces.

Anti-Harassment Training Does Not Work

It is fair to say that in a toxic workplace culture where there is a lot of conflict, disgruntled employees, and bosses who bully the employees, anti-harassment training will not, on its own, transform the organization into a positive and safe working environment. A positive workplace culture is where employees respect each other, there is trust among colleagues, people take responsibility for their actions, and will have a difficult conversation without denigrating anyone.

Anti-harassment training is not a new phenomenon. In fact, during the late 1960s and 1970s, there was a period of economic upheaval and immense social and political change. Out of this came the Civil Rights Movement, affirmative action legislation, and increases in workforce participation by minority groups, which resulted in significant increases in human relations training in the workplace, including human rights, equity, and diversity training. The Mental Health Commission of Canada highlights several factors leading to employers' responsibilities in creating a harassment-free workplace. These include labour laws, employment standards, employment contracts (common law), occupational health and safety; workers compensation legislation, law of torts (negligence), and human rights legislation. On December 9, 2009, an amendment to Ontario's Occupational Health and Safety Act (Bill 168) was declared, bringing violence and harassment within the framework of the employer's duty to provide a safe system of work. Alberta and the rest of the provinces followed thereafter. Despite compulsory anti-harassment training, the number of workplace harassment complaints continues to increase.

A survey by the Angus Reid Institute in 2018 indicated that 533 out of 1025 Canadian women experienced harassment in the workplace. The extent of the problem is reflected in formal reporting processes. For example, the Alberta Labour and Immigration Ministry reported receiving 811 allegations of harassment between 2018 and 2019, almost triple the number of 315 the previous year. In 2019, the Alberta Human Rights Commission reported 76 new cases of sexual harassment (a subset of harassment) in 2018-2019 in comparison to the 2017-2018 fiscal period. While anti-harassment training has proliferated over the past 10 years to address the problem, there is limited research regarding training effectiveness. A plausible explanation has been offered by a number of researchers over the past two decades, namely, there is a problem with the design of anti-harassment training programs.

Approaches to anti-harassment training vary widely across North America. Current teaching approaches to anti-harassment training have not been scrutinized. There are debates regarding program effectiveness, with some arguing that faulty program design is the problem and others maintain that ineffectiveness is due to poor human management. Others argue that the evidence of ineffectiveness is partially because studies had no control groups. In other words, it would be difficult (if not unethical) to provide anti-harassment training for one group in an organization and allow deviant behaviours to continue in another. Perhaps anti-harassment training is a mere symbolic gesture by employers to insulate themselves from legal liability. Antecol, Cobb-Clark, Bisom-Rapp, and many others scrutinize the anti-harassment training, yet they do not provide guidelines on ideal content, process, and/or design to improve the effectiveness of anti-harassment training.

While both governmental and non-governmental organizations in Canada have anti-harassment policies, a standard policy does not exist on anti-harassment training. In the absence of a standardized anti-harassment training design, training can take a variety of forms such as formal structured facilitation, lecture-based training, in-person facilitated workshops by a subject matter expert (SME) or HR practitioner, a group discussion, off the shelf-videos, case studies, and role playing. In the absence of a standardized training assessment tool, the resulting effectiveness of anti-harassment training includes mixed results and can be difficult to replicate. Furthermore, research into the effectiveness of anti-harassment training depends upon the researcher's conceptual framework, which not only indicates what counts as workplace harassment, but also what society deems as important to study (e.g., incivility, bullying, general workplace harassment, sexual harassment, or discrimination). Perry and Kulik assessed the effects of a sexual harassment awareness training video on college students in a mid-western city in the United States. The study showed that while video-based training increased knowledge and reduced the inappropriate behaviours of men, the most significant impact was only for those who had a high propensity to offend (tendency to sexually harass women). Moreover, the video-based training did not influence participants' long-term attitudes associated with the propensity to harass others.

Replicating a similar study in the workplace poses multiple challenges. First, how does one test for high propensity in the general workforce? Second, should a person have a high score with the propensity to offend, and who will have access to the information? Third, do scores get placed in the employee's personal file? Considering these limitations, along with the fact that very little is known from direct empirical evidence about how to design effective anti-harassment training, conducting a study opens the opportunity to explore alternative teaching approaches to anti-harassment training beyond off-the-shelf video training. One potentiality is to use a transformative whole person learning approach to improve the efficacy of anti-harassment program.

Anti-sexual Harassment Training

Sexual harassment is a subset of general workplace harassment. Far more expansive literature exists on sexual harassment in the workplace than other forms of harassment. Consequently, sexual harassment training is ubiquitous, with over 90% of all businesses conducting some form of sexual harassment training. In addition, training is a primary mechanism used by organizations to prevent harassment. Hence, teaching approaches and lessons learned from facilitating the prevention of sexual harassment can be applied to anti-harassment training.

Mark Roehling and Jason Huang provided the most comprehensive interdisciplinary review on the effectiveness of sexual-harassment training in the North American context. They explored and synthesized contemporary sexual harassment policies and training to identify gaps and call for researchers to adopt an integrated approach in researching the effectiveness of sexual harassment training. The results of their research confirm several observations, notably the ubiquitous nature of anti-harassment training but a lack of evidence that current program design leads to a reduction in harassment cases. For example, if an employer offers sexual harassment training merely to insulate themselves from legal liability, training will have very little impact. Although Roehling and Huang focused primarily on sexual harassment, their review, analysis, and recommendations remain relevant to other forms of workplace harassment including bullying and generalized workplace harassment. Consequently, the discussion which follows focuses on three key areas: definitional challenges, gaps in measuring the effectiveness of anti-harassment training, and suggestions for improving anti-harassment training outcomes.

Sexual Harassment Definitional Challenges

Sexual harassment is often divided into four categories: (a) legal, (b) social science, (c) organizational, and (d) individual. The legal category refers to legislation and being grounded in the law. For example, the Alberta Human Rights Commission (AHRC) defined sexual harassment as speech or behaviours that include unwelcome sexual advances, requests, physical contact, or gestures. These words or behaviours may be implied or expressed as threat of punishment for refusing to comply or inducement of reward for agreeing to comply. The AHRC identified sexual harassment as a form of gender discrimination. When I taught anti-harassment training, I drew on the legal definition of sexual harassment.

Sexual harassment definition is further divided into two sub-categories: quid pro quo (Latin term meaning *this for that*) and a hostile work environment. Quid pro quo sexual harassment involves positive or negative consequences in exchange for sexual favors. For example, a supervisor offers to give an employee a promotion if they fulfill sexual demands or demotes them if the person declines their offer. Quid pro quo threats generally impact employment-related decisions such as hiring, promotion, and termination. A hostile work environment, on the other hand, involves sex-related conduct that unreasonably interferes with an individual's work performance or creates an intimidating, hostile, or offensive working environment.

Social scientists offer a more expansive definition of sexual harassment. Aside from a sociological understanding of the phenomenon, also factored in are psychological aspects that include a person's perception of what constitutes inappropriate, demeaning, deregulatory, and humiliating actions. For example, if an employee shares a dirty joke in the workplace where all employees can hear, it may be defined and labelled differently. The comments may be interpreted as gender-based sexual harassment and/or lead to a hostile work environment. Additionally, other variations of sexual harassment exist such as unwanted sexual attention and sexual coercion. Much overlap exists in the definitions, as the boundaries are often blurred and difficult to demarcate into a specific category and are interpreted differently by law, social scientists, organizations, and individuals. Researchers and practitioners need to pay attention to varying definitions to determine program objectives, program design, and evaluation of results from workplace anti-harassment training.

There is consistent evidence that sexual harassment training increases awareness and that men are more likely to benefit from sexual harassment training, and that experiential methods are better than a passive reception of information, as participant involvement is crucial for successful training outcomes. Consequently, positive behavioral modeling is important if organizations want to create a respectful workplace free from harassment of any kind. This is to say that a sexual harassment complaint must be attended to immediately. In my experience, I responded to the complainant immediately acknowledging that I received the complaint. I ensured them that I secured an external investigator immediately to ensure a non-bias investigation. There should be no retaliation toward the complainant and managers should exercise strict confidentially until the investigation is complete. While sexual harassment training is essential, there needs to be a teaching design that increases the learner's knowledge, as well as shifts attitudes and behaviours around anti-harassment.

Gaps in Anti-harassment Training

Organizations have been providing some type of training to prevent disrespectful and uncivil behaviours in the workplace; however, the training has been mostly ineffective. Hence, there have been calls for educational approaches used in anti-harassment training to be scrutinized for their effectiveness. Some argue the ineffectiveness of anti-harassment training is because of poor human management; others have argued that ineffectiveness is because of faulty program design. In general terms, it can be argued that anti-harassment training is similar to other corporate training aligned with a cognitive and rational framework and approaches favoring the mind-intellect that overlook embodied participants who use emotions, sensations in the body, and spirit to make sense of their experiences. A facilitator working within the cognitive and rational framework will work toward developing participants' intellect and reasoning and perceive learning as constructed, rational, linear, and cyclical. Cognitive and rational methods and practices for anti-harassment training include challenging core beliefs and guiding learners to construct new concepts or mental maps using rational thinking and reasoning. While these techniques are much needed, scholars advocate for exploring innovative anti-harassment program design that exists beyond traditional compliance efforts.

Gaps in Measuring the Effectiveness of Sexual Harassment Training

Anti-harassment training in the workplace remains under scrutiny because of a heightened awareness of the issues and an increasing drive to provide basic information about the detrimental impact of disrespectful behaviours on individuals and organizations. However, there are immense challenges in measuring the frequency of incidents in a workplace and proving claims that sexual-harassment training reduces harassment in the workplace. Fragmented approaches in data collection at the organizational level, and the absence of a national databank in the Canadian context, make measuring the prevalence of harassment difficult. While the United States has a national databank and generous resources dedicated to the cause, nevertheless, making concrete claims that anti-harassment training reduces harassment remains elusive.

If the main goal of anti-harassment training is to increase skills and knowledge, and impact behaviour along with preventing harassment from happening in the first place, no comprehensive study to date addresses these challenges. The difficulty of measuring the effectiveness of sexual harassment training is two-fold. First, legal cases and those studying the phenomenon often fail to declare their specific definition, and second, there are methodological challenges such as relying on the opinion of college students' reactions to training while overlooking trainees' characteristics and the organizational context. *Trainees' characteristics* refers to aspects that trainees bring to the situation, such as previous knowledge, experiences, skills, abilities, attitudes, personality traits, motivations, demographics, and expectations. *Organizational context* refers to work environment and situational environment that include workplace morale, productivity, turnover, and layoffs.

As part of organizational context, anti-harassment program design also needs to be considered. For example, if a corporate anti-harassment program includes a PowerPoint lecture and having the employees read a handbook on anti-harassment policy and procedures, this may be *check the training box*, but may have little impact. In the case of sexual harassment, anti-harassment training may reinforce gender stereotypes and even backfire. There are several landmark decisions in the United States that solidified the need for employers to have mandatory sexual harassment training. One aspect of these decisions was in response to the *good faith* defense. A good faith defense is a legal defense where the employer suggests that they provided the necessary anti-harassment training which absolves them of responsibility should incidents of harassment continue in the workplace. To counter the good faith defense, the US Equal Employment Opportunity Commission (EEOC) in 2019 mandated a minimum of 2 hours mandatory training for all supervisors or employers who employ 50 people or more. In addition, training must be interactive and cover legal definitions of harassment. Although the AHRC in 2019 suggested mandatory training for companies with over 50 employees, they do not provide guidelines for anti-harassment program design.

While the AHRC conducts regular follow-up on the effectiveness of training via online surveys to all employers who participated in the Commission's training, however, no mandated guidelines exist for organizations to initiate their own training (from an in-house or an external consultant) without the involvement of the Commission. In any case, employers cannot simply provide a policy on paper; the policy must be effective in practice through tracking the number of complaints and measuring the number of complaints after anti-harassment training.

In my experience as a facilitator, anti-harassment training is rooted in the corporate anti-harassment policy and is a collaboration between administration, unions, and management. The policy highlights definitions of personal harassment, sexual harassment, and discrimination. Personal harassment is conduct that is unwelcome, uninvited, may be verbal, non-verbal, physical, tends to interfere with the employees' work performance, and creates an intimidating or hostile work environment. Sexual harassment behavior characterized by the making of unwelcome and inappropriate sexual remarks or physical advances in a workplace or other professional or social situation. Discrimination is an action or a decision that treats a person or a group badly for reasons such as their race, age, or ability.

These reasons, also called grounds, are protected under the Canadian Human Rights Act. It is noteworthy the anti-harassment policy highlights two mechanisms for employees to resolve complaints informally and formally. The informal complaint resolution involves the person who is experiencing harassment to make the situation known to the other person as constructively as possible to resolve the situation. If the problem persists, however, the complainant has the option to file a formal complaint and request an impartial investigation by a third party. In my workplace, labour relations consultants within the organization investigated personal harassment cases and an external investigator investigated discrimination cases. In principle, investigation should be conducted in a confidential manner; however, the investigation report is forwarded to the area manager where the complaint originated. Even in cases where an allegation is substantiated, the area manager is not obligated to follow the recommendations and in fact can modify, change, or disregard the recommendation. All final decisions rested with the area manager, and there was no appeal process.

The main purpose of training was to increase awareness of workplace diversity, as well as to develop and enhance skills among employees to recognize their biases, assumptions, and legal outcomes of discriminatory conduct. The goal was to create an environment that is free from bullying, harassment, and discrimination.

I trained thousands of employees over the course of 9 years. My teaching approach is best described as traditional. I served as the Subject Matter Expert (SME) in the classroom, lectured, provided a PowerPoint presentation, case studies, instructional videos, hosted discussions, and answered questions. I started each class by first introducing myself, and as part of an ice breaker, asked participants to share their names, a brief description of their positions, and something unique about them that other employees potentially did not know. The purpose of the ice breaker was to help participants get to know each other, promote interactions, and build trust.

In my experience, most participants arrived at class on time, appeared curious, asked questions, shared their personal narratives, participated in group activities, and were open-minded and respectful. On the other hand, a number of participants came in late without an excuse, appeared disinterested, were disrespectful, and some were openly hostile. At times, there was much tension in the room; participants did not talk with each other, averted eye contact with me, and did not participate in classroom activities. Countless participants complained about the mandatory requirement and claimed that training would not reduce harassment, citing a variety of reasons including bullying bosses, supervisors lacking mediation skills, toxic work culture, supervisors protecting the harassers, and retaliation against the complainant through either demotion, discipline, firing, salary reduction, or job or shift reassignment. Although the anti-harassment policy and procedure provided clear statements about behaviour that is unacceptable and guidelines on complaint resolution processes, bullying, harassment, and discrimination continue to hold different meanings to different employees.

Improving Anti-harassment Training Outcomes

The first task for a program administrator is to declare the working definition of harassment at the start of an anti-harassment training program. For example, the question to ask is: Will the training focus strictly on a legal definition or invoke an expansive behaviour-based definition of workplace harassment? Organizations committed to creating a psychologically safe working culture should move beyond providing the legal definition.

The second task is to align the working definition with training objectives, content, design, process, and evaluation. Hence, if the goal is change in behaviours, how will the program administrators ensure that participants increased their knowledge and applied the new knowledge seamlessly, thereby reducing workplace harassment. Third, the employer must explore attitudes, myth endorsement, and motivation, as well as the reasons for cynicism toward anti-harassment training. This is to say that the employer should inquire the reasons for resistance to anti-harassment training.

Content design should include legal definitions, case studies, interaction with participants, and subsequent course evaluation. Participants' feedback post-workshop is valuable in gauging whether training increased knowledge; however, the immediate feedback speaks to the *temporal aspect* of training. What remains is the need for intermediate and long-term program evaluation and measurement to determine if a decrease in harassment and litigation cases exist. Finally, anti-harassment training evaluation should establish organizational impact; for example, linking anti-harassment training to an increase in productivity, a lower turnover, and a higher return on investment (ROI).

Drawing from research conducted in Canada, the United States, and Australia, there are a number of important factors and wise practices to be considered in developing an effective anti-harassment program:

- Workplace culture plays a crucial role in training effectiveness. Gauge the workplace culture. Determine if the organization is ready for change.

- Workers' attitudes will shift if they feel the organization is ethical and will take complaints seriously.

- Leaders should model civil and respectful workplace behaviours.

- All workers should be asked to reflect on ways in which their behaviours impact others.

- Most workers do not report incidents because they feel nothing will be done; hence, investigate complaints thoroughly, and in a timely manner. If the complaint is against a supervisor or manager, ensure the investigation is conducted by an independent investigator.

- Offering training for strategic reasons is a better option than for mere compliance.

- An organization's climate, policies, and practices impact training effectiveness.

- Training must meet the needs of both the individual and organization.

- Development of an anti-harassment policy and a corporate-wide anti-harassment training program should be combined with a robust internal grievance procedure.

- Conduct a pre- and post-workshop evaluation of participants to gauge their level of knowledge about the topic and their perceptions post-training to gauge transfer of skills. Training is effective when there is an anti-harassment policy and grievance process.

- Specify the objectives of training.

- Select appropriate training techniques in the context where training takes place.

- Active participation is crucial as it produces greater attitudinal change than passive reception of information.

- If the goal of training is attitudinal and behavioral changes, then combine anti-harassment videos with experiential methods, role play, and group discussion.

Anti-Harassment Training Does Not Work

Anti-harassment training is seen as a panacea for all the problems; however, such programs are also not always evaluated for their effectiveness and long-term impact. There are several proposed training strategies to enhance anti-harassment training; however, there are many challenges in developing a standardized anti-harassment training program for a diverse set of people and contexts. First, people respond differently to training. Hence, while knowing the characteristics of participants is valuable, it is not always feasible. However, a pretest to gauge learner / worker's knowledge is helpful.

Second, there is a lack of systemically evaluated sexual harassment training programs (in fact, Perry and his associates claim there are only nine studies to date). Hence, it is difficult to predict if applying wise practices will lead to better results.

Third, considering individual beliefs and attitudes are difficult to change, a challenge for organizations is in designing anti-harassment training programs that ultimately lead to a reduction in the incidence of workplace harassment to result in a long-term impact.

CHAPTER THREE
WORKPLACE LEARNING

Terminology is both liberating and restrictive. On the one hand, we need terms and definitions to ensure that we are talking about the same thing. So, when I refer to a pen or a pencil, you can perhaps visualize a black ink pen or a lead pencil. Things are not that simple when we talk about the complex topic of workplace learning. Suffice it to say that workplace learning is often geared toward enhancing workplace process, procedures, and efficiencies. Workplace learning can be best explained as an interdisciplinary field that borrows from a variety of other domains such as adult education, sociology, psychology, and economics.

In the field of workplace learning, the terms *learning* and *training* are often used interchangeably. It is important to distinguish between these two terms. According to Jarvis, learning refers to knowledge or skills acquired by instruction, self-discovery, reading, experience, mentorship, and self-reflection resulting in a long-lasting behaviour shift. Training is acquisition of a specific useful competency for a specific job. While my own preference is for *learning*, for reasons that I will explain later, the term *training* is most frequently used to describe specific kinds of programs in the workplace. Contemporary discussion about workplace learning has to be situated within historical, social, political, and economic contexts that reveal both continuity and change over the last 50 years. Exploring the history of workplace learning opens consideration for exploring motivation and philosophy embedded in current anti-harassment training design.

History of Workplace Learning

The history of work can be traced back over 3000 years, starting with hunters and gatherers, followed by an agrarian economy, which eventually gave way to the industrial economy, to mass-production, the assembly line, and later to the knowledge economy and a mobile workforce. As societies became more complex, workplace learning evolved beyond learning job-specific skills (as in the first Industrial Revolution) to solving work-related problems (development of the field of human resources (HR) and related compliance training). It is reasonable to conclude that workplace learning is both an individual activity and a social phenomenon that goes beyond individual learning to changing groups and organizations.

The Industrial Revolution of the late 1700s marked the introduction of mechanization of manufacturing using steam power. Mechanical production led to a rise in opportunity for apprenticeships in crafts and trades, hence the increase of guilds and advanced skills needed to operate machinery. The Industrial Revolution also served as a catalyst for formal schooling and gradually led to pre-service occupational courses designed to prepare people for generic aspects of occupations. By the 1800s, the second phase of the Industrial Revolution introduced the hallmark for mechanized manufacturing equipment and division of labour and electrification, resulting in training workers to operate new machinery. Companies opened factory schools that were possibly the first formal programs of instruction in the workplace.

Following this period, Fredrick Taylor and Frank Gilbert introduced a scientific management system that became known as Scientific Taylorism, Scientific Management, and often simply as Taylorism. The premise behind Taylorism was to break down every action, job, or task into small and simple segments to determine the best way to improve efficiency and reduce workers' strain. Workplace training under Taylorism focused on standardization and efficiency. Workplace training in the above context meant teaching technical skills and meeting business objectives.

The Western Electric Company in the 1920s and 1930s commissioned research to explore working conditions and their impact on workers' behaviour and attitude, resulting in the *Hawthorne Effect*. The Hawthorne Effect revealed that a variety of physical, economic, and social variables can improve worker productivity. Although these experiments garnered significant criticism, the research was arguably the first to identify human psychological and social variables such as attitude and motivation, and their impact on team development and productivity. Consequently, the 1920s marked the introduction of principles of Total Quality Management (TQM) that essentially focused on producing quality work and, for the first time, shifted the focus from operational needs to improving service to customers.

Starting in the 1920s, workplace learning shifted to include hard and soft skills. Soft skills are interpersonal qualities, also known as people skills and personal attributes. The development of soft skills is akin to anti-harassment training in that it teaches learners about communication and conflict resolution skills. By the 1950s, the principles of TQM transformed human resource development (HRD), which led to prioritizing the alignment of training and development with strategic business objectives and goals. During the 1960s, the third Industrial Revolution took place, referred to as the Digital Revolution when the information technology (IT) industry became integrated in manufacturing. The rapid advancement in technologies resulted in a proliferation of the field of HRD and organizational development in approaches to work. It was during this period that Theodore Schultz developed the human capital theory of economic growth, which declared that human capital is most likely to accelerate economic growth, becoming highly influential in workforce training. During this period, early anti-harassment training efforts centered on legislation and compliance.

The late 1960s and the 1970s was a period of economic upheaval and immense social and political change. From this came the Civil Rights' movement, affirmative action legislation, and increases in workforce participation by minority groups, which resulted in significant increases in human relations training in the workplace including human rights, equity, and diversity training. The United States legislated mandatory anti-harassment training, as did Canada. Preventing harassment became a national interest and employers and employees shared responsibility for creating a respectful workplace.

By the late 1970s, workplace training took yet another turn; this time there was push-back against human relations training (soft skills) toward skills-based and life-skills training.

The growing influence of human capital theory in adult education and workplace learning drove a managerial approach to workplace learning grounded in the principles of economic return on investment (ROI), rather than being transformative. During the 1990s, rapid globalization, political changes, and competition led to mergers and the acquisition of new markets and global competition that demanded a skilled labour force, further changing the face of workplace learning. Globalization meant increasing reliance on a temporary workforce, as well as partnering with colleges and businesses to provide this training. Once again workplace learning linked to organizational and global competitiveness. Technological and organizational developments within a competitive environment resulted in increased attention for training as a determinant for human capital. Under the human capital rubric, workplace training supported skills workers required for industry. The social, political, and economic drivers served as catalysts for developing a knowledge-based economy, and HRD moved toward an increased reliance on the market model as a way of framing its practice.

The knowledge based economy led to the classification of the fourth Industrial Revolution, leading to the creation of a mobile worker. While the second Industrial Revolution was characterized as mass production followed by automation, computers, and electronics, the fourth Industrial Revolution in the 1990s was characterized by a range of new technologies fusing the physical, digital, and biological worlds, and impacting all disciplines, economies, and industries, including significant impact on the nature of workplace learning. The advent of a mobile worker, someone who works in more than one place, travels as part of their job, and uses mobile devices as part of their job, is the new norm. More than two-thirds of Canadian employees already do some of their work each week outside the office, and the expectation is for this trend to grow over the coming years as mobile devices proliferate and employers encourage their use. The 2020 Global Pandemic necessitated many organizations to move employees' training online. It can be argued that this influenced workplace training by stressing *head training* rather than embodied, experiential, and whole person learning. These trends need to be considered in the future design of anti-harassment training. For example, in 2017, the Equal Employment Opportunity Commission (EEOC), suggested that the most effective anti-harassment training is conducted live, is expert-led, and lasts a minimum of 4 hours. The EEOC also suggests that video and online training strategies do not work to change behaviour.

How Workplace Learning Has Evolved

Providing clear, concise definitions and explanations of concepts used in the book poses challenges. The burgeoning interest in workplace learning since the 1970s engaged researchers across diverse fields, including education, psychology, sociology, labour process studies, economics, organizational studies, HRD, business, and management. There are multiple ways to conceptualize a working location / place from the most obvious physical location to a more esoteric spiritual location, and more recently, virtual location. The term *workplace* commonly refers to the physical location where one works. A workplace is understood to include the physical location, shared meaning, ideas, behaviours, and attitudes that determine the working environment and relationship.

Workplace learning is a contested field of inquiry. For example, without a critical examination *workplace learning* might mean different things to academics and practitioners. Considering that the term *workplace learning* includes definitions used in multiple ways by different groups with varied interests, it is difficult to arrive at a single definition or paradigm that researchers and practitioners support and agree upon universally. Worker / learner and *workplace* are inextricably interdependent. The term *learning* in most people's vernacular is used ubiquitously and often interchangeably with terms such as *education* and *training*. Learning can take the form of acquisition, upgrading, and updating of job-specific skills, as well as the strengthening of soft skills, such as communication, critical thinking, and problem-solving abilities. Learning is a *process* that leads to change, which occurs as a result of experience, and increases the potential for improved performance and future learning.

These definitions are not absolute but rather fluid, as they evolve continually. For example, some authors view education as a broader category than learning and training, suggesting that education assists learners in opening their identities and exploring new ways of being. Learning is also defined as an ongoing process defined as *relatively permanent change in behaviour, cognition, or affect*. While workplace learning remains commonly used, other terms also used include work-based learning, learning in the workplace, training, HRD, learning, and development, workplace-based learning, work-related learning, and learning at work. Some scholars integrate learning with working and working with learning. Workplace learning includes the conception of individuals learning in a structured workplace, involving deliberate and conscious learning activities to reflect on actual workplace experiences. In addition, workplace learning can also be characterized as developmental activities and education efforts within the organization to help establish a culture of organizational learning. Some authors have invoked terms such as *work-based learning* to mean the learning of individuals and the organization. Supporting this idea, others propose that workplace learning involves the process of reasoned learning towards desirable outcomes for the individual and the organization. Yet others contend that the primary unit of workplace learning is the individual and not necessarily the organization. Nonetheless, workplace learning cannot be separated from the working context in which it occurs. In addition, workers / learners learn from each other and are interdependent.

Workplace learning can also be conceptualized as a way in which individuals or groups acquire, interpret, reorganize, change, or assimilate related information, skills, and feelings. Hence, workplace learning is the primary way in which people construct meaning in their personal and shared organizations. In brief, workplace learning includes the definition either as learning for self, learning for organization, or both. Work and learning are not distinct entities. Workplaces afford opportunities for employee learning through interactions with other workers and their day-to-day work activities. In addition, workplace learning can be also defined as a highly social activity that requires interaction and dialogue that make learning necessary and involves reflection on past experiences and planning for future activities. It is worth noting people bring their histories, social location, intersectionality (Crenshaw, 1991), motivation, self-efficacy, previous experiences, knowledge, and skill(s). Hence, trainees' characteristics should be factored into an anti-harassment training workshop.

Forms of Workplace Learning

Sometimes learning cannot be designed; it happens naturally through experience and practice. Hence, learning can happen with or without design. An opposing view is that learning is an intentional, cognitive, and embodied activity that involves various types of processes, such as formal, structured, non-formal (non-credentialed), and informal, incidental, tacit, experiential, and reflexive, and peripheral learning. Formal workplace learning is generally structured (in terms of learning objectives and time) and leads to certification. Formal workplace learning occurs in a context not provided by an education or training institution and typically does not lead to certification. However, this type of learning does include structure in terms of learning objectives, learning time, and support. Informal learning is intentional but often at the discretion of the learner. In other words, it is self-directed and occurs through normal day-to-day activities, which may include interaction with other employees, observation, and mentorship. Incidental learning is a subset of informal learning, as training lacks formal structure, and the learner may not have the intention to learn. Conceptualized, workplace learning includes (a) learning that occurs inter-psychologically through participation in social practices (or locations) such as workplaces; (b) workers learn by engaging in everyday routine activities, thereby gaining new skills and refining existing knowledge; hence, they create new knowledge; (c) workers receive guidance from more experienced co-workers leading to deeper understanding than learning in a structured classroom; (d) participation and guidance afforded to workers are shaped by workplace values, hierarchies, group affiliations, personal relations; and (e) simply offering learning opportunities is insufficient. Because learning occurs in the workplace informally, workplaces should consider providing guidance and support on an on-going basis.

In addition, there are many forms of workplace learning that include: self-directed learning, individual learning, learning within a team or group, community of practice, in-house workplace-sponsored training, tuition reimbursement programs commonly offered through third-party educational institutions, and a professional licensing body, to name a few. Furthermore, in-house HR practitioners, external SMEs, or consultants may offer *off the shelf* or customized training. Workplace learning is the way in which individuals or groups acquire, interpret, reorganize, change or assimilate a related cluster of information, skills, and feelings. It is also primary to the way in which people construct meaning in their personal and shared organizational lives. Within the context of workplace learning, anti-harassment training is about constructing new knowledge, re-interpreting information, reorganizing meaning, responding to change, and changing behaviours.

Future of Workplace Learning

Undoubtedly, the nature of work has shifted significantly since the first Industrial Revolution, and the world of work has changed drastically. With new technologies and modes of workplace organization, certain tendencies are expected to continue—workplaces will serve as potential sites of learning, employers will be motivated to train employees for particular skills in the workplace, and the government's interest in increasing workplace skills and capacity for innovation to compete in the global marketplace will not change. We as a society need to critically think about the future of workplace learning, including what might be potentially new roles for the instructor. Davenport (2006) believed that training will (a) become more learner centered; (b) be tailored to both individual and company needs; (c) shift technology (for example, nanotechnology and artificial intelligence (AI)) that will ultimately call for training and retraining of workers; (d) be self-directed learning; (e) become a naturally observed practice in everyday work processes; and (f) be on-going rather than discrete learning activities and events. In terms of the role of the instructor in the future, instructors will still be required to train in the workplace; however, their role will be predominantly that of a facilitator / guided-support instructor; expectations will include managing changing technology and offering training and other learning opportunities to individuals using mobile devices (including smart phones and laptops) and social media platforms. However, we should ensure that the social media platforms include games, case studies, and role play, otherwise training will be a one-way street, teacher-led and compliance-focused. While many authors provide comprehensive analysis of the past and ideas around training and development, what remains lacking are clear guidelines regarding program design in general or any specific approach in teaching anti-harassment training. Unquestionably, training in the paid workplace is essential and contributes to an organization's competitiveness. At this juncture, it is useful to further explore the meanings and definitions attached to workplace learning.

CHAPTER FOUR
SOCIAL LOCATION, POSITIONALITY, AND INTERSECTIONALITY

All of us who are interested in making changes in a workplace to ensure a safe, respectful environment come with our own backgrounds. An educator for over 25 years, I have observed that many participants come to the anti-harassment workshops seeking tools and techniques but are hesitant to explore the identities, mindset, and prejudices they hold. Many profess to be objective, unbiased, and neutral and claim to treat everyone the same. I believe that nobody can ever claim to be 100% unbiased, objective, and neutral. As human beings, we are born into a world that existed prior to our existence. We learn through both direct and indirect observation, experiences, and through our senses. Therefore, before I start a workshop, I spend significant time getting to know the participants and the lenses they bring to the workshop and in creating a psychologically safe space for them to explore who they are. Suffice it to say that before we get to tools and techniques, we need to interrogate our socialization.

My situation is similar in that the early socialization by my parents, siblings, peers in school, friends, relatives, acquaintances, and all forms of media has shaped my thinking, feelings, and being. Therefore, what I write in this book is filtered through these lenses; albeit I made every attempt to examine how I formed certain assumptions and acquired many biases along the way. It is important for me to share my identities and experiences, and to model how sharing about our identities does not feel like a daunting task, but rather a method by which we can build rapport and examine how our identities influence and shape the work we do.

Take adult education and learning as an example. I grew up in three different countries: Saudi Arabia, Pakistan, and Canada. I went to Christian schools up until I was 7 years old. The teachers were strict when it came to uniform, punctuality, and discipline in the classroom. My undergraduate days in Canada were not much different. I went to classes with over 50 students, the instructor lectured, and I took notes. Exams were usually made up of multiple choice questions. There was not much interaction between instructor and students. It was not until I was in my graduate studies that I realized the importance of dialogue between the instructor, student, and peers. For the longest time I thought teaching was a one-way communication and participants were supposed to take the information and apply the knowledge seamlessly. Over the course of many years, trials, and tribulation and working in anti-harassment training and research, I discovered that acquiring knowledge is one thing, but acquiring skills and then applying them in the workplace context poses multiple challenges. For instance, it is one thing to know that spreading malicious gossip and

Social Location, Positionality, and Intersectionality

publicly humiliating a co-worker is harmful to the individual; it is another challenge to stop such behaviour that could potentially create a toxic work culture. Bullying, harassment, and discrimination are rampant in many workplaces. Many times, the workers are not aware of how their behaviour impacts another person. Other times, the perpetrator is told how their behaviour is having a negative impact on their subordinate and colleagues, yet they refuse to change their behaviours.

Where do we start? Let us begin with exploring who we are and the lenses or filters through which we see the world. Our identities, socialization, and mindsets matter in training help us to uncover our values, beliefs, and assumptions. I discovered a useful framework that helped me understand some of my biases and assumptions. The framework uses tools such as social identity, location, and intersectionality. This framework can be useful for trainers and managers to be self-reflective, know who they are, and how they interpret the world. In addition, self-reflection potentially leads to understanding power relations embedded in the workplace and how we approach teaching. A better understanding of ourselves and how we interpret the world leads to better rapport with employees and potentially helps to build better relationships with loved ones and acquaintances.

An individual's social location is defined as the combination of factors including gender, race, social class, age, ability, religion, sexual orientation, and geographic location. These factors shape our mindset, beliefs, and values. Social location is particular to everyone and not always the same for any two individuals. A Black woman's experience will be different than mine even though we are both non-Whites.

Anti-Harassment Training Does Not Work

Positionality refers to one's stance in relation to the social and political context where they live and work. My experience as a non-White settler in Canada has resulted in a heightened awareness of ways in which persons of colour are depicted in the media, the experiences that I share with other persons of colour, and my position in comparison to the White European Canadian.

Intersectionality is another tool for understanding how aspects of a person's social and political identities combine to create different modes of discrimination and privilege. In other words, while I have experienced racial discrimination firsthand, I also have tremendous privileges: I acquired my education in Canada, I am able-bodied, middle class, and cis-gender. The way I view and interpret the social world is impacted by where, when, and how I am socially located and the position from which I see the world around me.

I identify as a 50-year-old, able-bodied, middle-class, heterosexual, cis-gender (I identify with the sex assigned at birth), South Asian / Indian woman of colour. The second layer highlights certain advantages and concerns I have. For instance, I have formal education and my middle-class status affords physical safety. While I am rooted in my social identity as a South Asian / Indian woman of colour I am also hypersensitive to racism. As a Canadian citizen, I enjoy certain freedoms and have the right to vote. As a heterosexual, I am generally socially accepted, and I do not have to worry about ensuring my gender is represented on a government form. Being able-bodied, I have access to physical spaces, I do not need to request accommodation. As cis-gender, I do not have to worry about pronouns. Any change in one of these categories can skew my social location and therefore change my intersectionality with parts of society that influence my thoughts and feelings.

The following illustration captures my social location and intersectionality and I have added another layer that I call thoughts, feelings, and emotions. This framework can be used by anyone (see Figure 1).

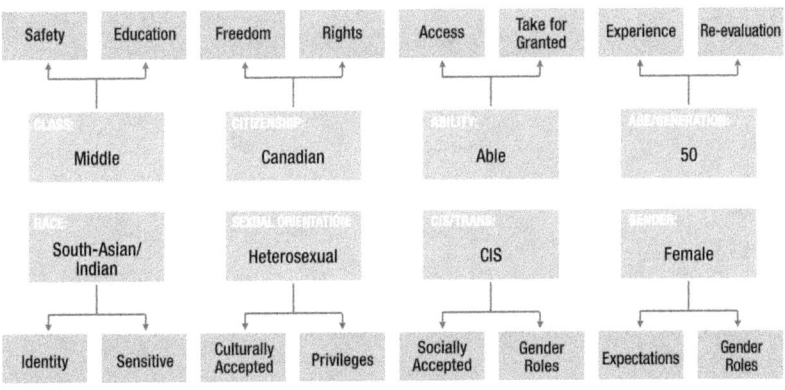

Figure 1: Social Location and Intersectionality

Sharing one's background makes them vulnerable, but I think that it is imperative that leaders and trainers should create a safe space to share their background, social identity, location, and intersectionality so that they can connect with the participants.

CHAPTER FIVE
TRANSFORMATIVE LEARNING AND ANTI-HARASSMENT TRAINING

Transformative learning (TL) is learning that leads to a significant change and a substantial shift in how people think, feel, and learn in a long-lasting way, as demonstrated in the following vignette:

> I grew up in a nuclear family with influences from two religions. My mother practiced Islam and I attended a Catholic school during my primary years. The Islamic and Catholic influences, along with the socialization from by parents, media, and peers, left an impression on me and I internalized the nuclear family as a normative reality. I thought there were only two genders in the world, male and female, and sex and gender meant the same thing. My early socialization and experiences shaped my worldview. I took for granted these views until I took a course in

anthropology where I took part in a role play, listened to the narratives of sexual minorities, and gained a larger understanding of the norms of sexual orientation in relation to family dimensions.

The role play was simple; however, it had a huge impact on me. At first, the instructor did not provide the purpose of the activity, he simply asked all students to make two rows and referred to the groups as Group A and Group B. He sat at his desk pretending to conduct some sort of a need's assessment, then he asked each student to step forward. He asked each student a few questions. I have no idea what he asked the student ahead of me but when it was my turn, he asked me for my name, address, and how I would like to be identified. At first, I did not understand what he meant so I inquired, and he clarified "Would you like be referred to as he / she / other?" I chuckled and stated, "She, obviously." Once he went through Group A and B, he instructed the students to form a group of four or five and share their observations with each other.

Two students in my group were visibly upset that the instructor had asked students to share their pronouns, while others in my group wanted to openly discuss sexual identity and expression. A couple of students talked about being bullied in high school because they either looked different (they did not dress according to their assigned gender) and/or had trouble fitting in with their peers because they did not participate in sports. After the debrief, the instructor continued the lecture and shared more information about the social construction of gender. The instructor posed a question to the group. He asked, "How would you feel had I assigned a gender to each group without your consent?" The question led me to critically examine my essentialist views and biases. The question also shifted the energy in my body. I felt my heart sink, my heart rate slowed down, and my breathing became shallow. My heart was aching for students who expressed feeling isolated and bullied because they did not identify with the gender they were assigned at birth.

At that time, I could not make sense of what was happening for me but in retrospect, I can say that the experience of standing in the line, listening to the students' lived experiences, and the professor explaining the social construction of sex, gender, and gender identity, shifted my thinking and being. Sometimes putting feelings into words is challenging, but the best way to describe my experience that day is to say that I reconnected with my body and started to pay attention to bodily sensations. While I was raised to pay attention to the messages from the body (anxiety, heaviness in the chest, heart rate, blood pressure, headache, tightness in the jaw, butterflies in the stomach, and back pain) by my maternal uncle, later in life as I grew older, I became disconnected from the body; however, the anthropology class I just described was a good reminder to return to the wisdom of the body. Looking back, the experience was personally transformative and changed my practice. For example, I am drawn to transformative learning and critical theory.

By having students share their personal experiences through critical inquiry and dialogue, physical movement, and role play, the instructor precipitated reflection, invoked feelings, and deep emotions in the students, and thereby moved the information from the head to the body. My worldview shifted, and I understood then that the principles of transformative learning, as illustrated in the vignette is a whole person (mind, body, and spirit) model that can be applied to teaching anti-harassment training. The goal of anti-harassment training is to share an organization's policy, complaint resolution processes, and reduce workplace conflicts. We need a different approach to ensure that information is internalized and moves from the head to the heart and hands, resulting in a shift in an individual's perspective. Transformative learning provides the language and tools such as critical dialogue and self-reflection that opens the possibility of moving information from the head to the heart and hands.

Roots of Transformative Learning

In 1968, a Brazilian educator and philosopher Paulo Freire published *Pedagogy of the Oppressed* which became a key part of the critical pedagogy (science of teaching), or critical education movement. Transformative learning began with two significant developments within the adult education tradition. Critical education is a philosophy of education promoting personal transformation and social change, and two theories, critical pedagogy and critical social theory arose as a result. Both theories inform transformative learning.

Jack Mezirow, an American sociologist, first described the concept of transformation and transformative learning during the 1970s, while he was studying women's experiences in the United States returning to post-secondary study or the workplace after an extended period. The theory has been expanded, scrutinized, and revised over the last four decades. The twentieth century American educator John Dewey, perceived learning as a psychological process, which has purpose, is directional and ultimately connected to the learner's life; hence, experience is central to adult learning and education. Transformative learning theory is grounded in this rich tradition and is placed on a continuum of the humanistic, psychological, experiential learning traditions, and critical thought. Accordingly, Jack Mezirow conceptualizes learning as developmental, and experience plays a central role. Thereby, transformative learning is understood as the process of using a prior interpretation to construe a new or revised interpretation of the meaning of one's experience to guide future action.

Building further on these ideas, Mezirow identified three types of learning: instrumental, communicative / dialogical, and self-reflective. Instrumental learning is learning through task-oriented problem solving and determining cause and effect. A communicative or dialogical approach seeks guidance from experts, talks with co-workers and other learners, and arrives at the best way to reach a goal. Self-reflective learning involves thinking independently and questioning and redefining the problem. Likewise, a critical pedagogical approach in teaching anti-harassment must include tapping into a learner / worker's experience, helping them to revise prior meanings while using these three types of learning.

Drawing on Paulo Freire's work, the first strand of transformative learning is *consciousness raising*, which aims to raise critical consciousness, develop critical perspectives, and challenge the status quo. The purpose is to analyze situations, pose problems, pose questions, learn about social systems, structures, and power differentials that contribute to inequality and oppression and ultimately promote political liberation from oppression. The role of the educator is to facilitate a dialogue with learners and examine how structures and systems shape their cognition and influence how they perceive themselves and others in society. The second strand of transformative learning is the strategy of using *critical reflection to lead to a change in perspective.* This is to say that people sometimes make meaning of their lived experience without much thought or reflection. However, critical self-reflection, critical thinking about one's situation, and context leads to a shift in perspective.

Although transformation can occur through reflection, gradually or through acute social and/or personal crises, three essential components are required for structure transformation: (a) *centrality of experience,* (b) *critical reflection and objective,* and (c) *rational discourse.* However, I am modifying the formula: I am suggesting that the body and mind are connected, hence we can rely on the body, emotions, and spirit to guide our decisions. The starting point of transformation is the learner's experience and the topic under discussion. The first step is to recognize that experience is socially constructed; hence, it can be deconstructed, unlearned, and critically examined. The role of the facilitator is to disrupt the learner's worldview and arouse curiosity, perhaps arousing uncertainty about previously taken-for-granted interpretations of experiences. The second essential component toward structure transformation is critical reflection on assumptions and subjective reframing. This is to say that a learner should reflect on ways in which the culture has distorted meaning and put constraints on perceptions of perceived reality. The third essential component is discourse. Here the teacher and student engage in questioning the topic under discussion, weighing pros and cons, dialogue, negotiation of meaning, reflection, and ultimately transformation of the learner.

Mezirow frames the problem as follows: humans are born in a socio-cultural-political-economic-linguistic environment; they often uncritically adopt the environmental nuances and intentionally or unintentionally learn perspectives about themselves and the world. However, adult learners have the capability via critical thinking and critical discussion to see distortions in their beliefs, feelings, and attitudes. These experiences lead to a fundamental shift in how people see themselves and others, and ways in which they engage with the world. Hence, the role of transformative learning is to help learners to construe a new or revised interpretation of a situation to guide future action.

Critical Education

To apply the ideas of TL we use components of *critical pedagogy*—critical thinking, consciousness raising, critical dialogue, the discovery of new knowledge, collective action, praxis (reflection and action), and concern for social justice. Critical pedagogy goes beyond the surface meaning of a concept. This concept includes critical examination of dominant myths, traditional clichés, received wisdom, and public discourse to understand deeper meaning, social context, and hidden agendas behind an idea. Critical pedagogy is about learning, unlearning, re-learning, reflection, evaluation, and action, and ultimately examining the effect educators have on learners. While this theory is born in educational contexts, many of its theoretical forms apply in the workplace. Critical pedagogy includes examination of the ways in which people have been historically disadvantaged. For example, to suggest that workers have equal power in the organization and can resolve conflicts by simply approaching a disruptive or abusive person, describing their offensive behaviour, and asking the perpetrator to stop the behaviour, does not allow for critical reflection of *who actually has power to make change?* If the offending person is their supervisor, can a worker approach them and express how they make them feel excluded, disrespected, harassed, and bullied? If they do, what are the consequences?

In the traditional educational environment, a learner listens to a lecturing teacher and consumes decontextualized knowledge produced by the teacher, but this educational environment is limited because it negates learners' individual lived experiences, social location, and intersectionality. Learners are not empty containers into which educators place knowledge.

There are several concepts that are important to understanding critical pedagogy.

- **Dialogue.** Both teachers and learners come to the classroom socialized by the existing dominant culture and ideology, however they may come from different backgrounds and traditions. Dialogue is an invitation to explore issues collectively by allowing for each participant's life experience, their intersectionality with this workplace environment. Facilitators teaching anti-harassment training should take the time to understand participants' lived experiences with workplace harassment before bombarding learners with information about anti-harassment policy and procedures.

- **Critical inquiry** such as problem-posing. Humans are not *cognition in a casing*, and knowledge cannot exist apart from the body. Emotion, body, and spirit are part of the development of the intellect. Therefore, relying on lecture and sharing PowerPoint presentations, instructors limit participants' learning.

- **Praxis** is part of critical pedagogy and is defined as movement between reflecting and acting and interpreting a situation. When applied to anti-harassment training, the organization's policy and procedures are continuously adjusted based on the lived experiences of the workers.

- **Horizontal student-teacher relationships** is a vertical dyad relationship between teacher and student and is where the teacher teaches, and the student learns. The horizontal dyad model is when the teacher builds trust in the participants and creates a safe space for critical inquiry. The personal and social experiences merge and transformational learning occurs when both instructor and participants dialogue and co-create knowledge. The instructor is not the only expert in the classroom.

- **Self-reflection and consciousness raising.** Self-reflective learning involves thinking independently, questioning, and re-defining a problem. The instructor taps into participant experience, helps them to revise prior meanings. The instructor can guide the learner through dialogue and self-reflection. Consciousness raising aims to analyze situations, pose problems, ask questions to learn about the organization where people work and understand social systems, structures and power differentials that contribute to inequality. Participants ask themselves what is in their span of control and where and how they can influence the removal of systemic barriers.

- **Critical social theory (CST)** stresses a re-examination of societal structures and culture with a critical lens. The theory has two distinct meanings with different origins and histories, one originating in sociology and the other in literary criticism. Unlike traditional social theories that attempt to understand or explain a phenomenon, the role of CST is to dig below the surface understanding and uncover the assumptions that keep people from fully understanding how the world works. The goal is to ultimately critique and change society. When applied to teaching anti-harassment training, facilitators applying CST move beyond the nuts and bolts of anti-harassment policy to having an authentic conversation about the policy and complaint resolution processes and their effectiveness.

The role of the facilitator in teaching anti-harassment training is to facilitate a dialogue with learners to present and discuss anti-harassment policy and complaint resolution processes, examine ways in which conflict shows up, and workplace harassment occurs, and introduce a mechanism to resolve complaints and barriers in implementing the policy.

Critical self-reflection is part of critical pedagogy. People sometimes make meaning of their lived experience without much thought or reflection. However, critical self-reflection, critical thinking about one's situation, and context leads to a shift in perspective.

Perspective Transformation

Perspectives are made up of beliefs, values, and assumptions that people acquire through their life experiences. Perspectives, also known as points of view and outlooks, are akin to a set of lenses through which people see the world. One's perspectives or worldview, are essentially untested assumptions of reality. Perspective transformation is the process of becoming critically aware of how and why our assumptions have come to constrain the way we perceive and feel about our world; changing the structures of habitual expectation to make possible a more inclusive, discriminating, and integrating perspective; and finally, making choices or otherwise acting upon this new understanding. The facilitator can use a variety of tools to have participants reflect on their perspectives, such as asking participants to interrogate their emotions, feelings, and sensations in the body when certain issues are brought forth.

Frames of Reference

Frames of reference alludes to one's personal background and historical contexts that shape meaning and interpretation of their world. Nested within the frames of reference component are two categories: *meaning schemas* and *meaning perspectives*. Meaning schemas are made up of specific knowledge, beliefs, values, judgments, and feelings that constitute interpretations of experience. Meaning schemas go beyond habits and expectations that influence and shape people's behaviours or points of view. In fact, meaning schemas are altered when one critically reflects on the content of the problem and engages in problem-solving. Habits of mind are broad, abstract, oriented habitual ways of thinking, feeling, and acting influenced by assumptions that constitute a set of cultural, political, social, educational, and economic codes. *Point of view* is another name for meaning schema and is the constellation of belief, value judgment, attitude, and feelings that shape a particular interpretation. A key point worth noting is that habits of mind operate below human consciousness (commonly referred to as unconscious bias) while meaning schemas or points of view are conscious biases.

Structure Transformation

To put the above theories into context, suffice it to say that our social location, positionality, and intersectionality gives us a lens by which we see the world. Hence, a cis-gender, able-bodied, middle-class person might struggle with understanding the lived experiences of a racialized woman of colour living below poverty. The person in position of privilege and power might assume that education is an equalizer, and that people are poor by choice. Transformation alludes to a person shifting their lens from being closed-minded to open-minded and receptive to new ideas. To put it in different terms, the person in position of privilege and power realizes about how society is structured to favour those with higher education, with access to resources, and networking capabilities.

CHAPTER SIX
WHOLE PERSON LEARNING APPROACH

The whole person learning approach that I propose is a tailored approach in teaching anti-harassment workshops. The whole person approach is steadfast to the foundational tenets of transformative learning, including but not limited to, the significance of the learner's experience (social location, positionality, and intersectionality), conscientization or raising awareness, critical reflection, and critical dialogue. Workplace harassment is an emotionally charged topic, and traditional teaching methods such as sharing the anti-harassment policy, sharing a vignette, and fact giving is not sufficient. A learner's experience is a reasonable starting point to build new knowledge. This is to say that the facilitator should ask participants about their experience of workplace conflict, harassment, and conflict resolution. The facilitator should move beyond a rational dialogue and incorporate a discussion around feelings, emotions, and spirit. Emotions and feelings are interlinked and work as a *sieve*. How one receives, processes, stores, and retrieves information is filtered through the sieve. It is worth noting the learner may not always be conscious of the reasons for their reaction; hence, a facilitator can ask probing questions starting with *what are your thoughts,* how do you feel, do you sense strong emotions. Certain topics or subjects invoke strong emotions and feeling, and reactions can either motivate or impede learning. Print, speech, and visual cues are important; however, teaching approaches such as watching short film clips, documentaries, and expressing emotions and feelings through art, and storytelling, allow for deeper exploration of thoughts and emotions. Moreover, there are certain topics that can only be expressed imaginatively rather than conceptually.

We all have different learning styles and learners learn in multiple ways: *experiential, presentational, propositional, and practical.* Experiential learning is direct sensory contact with the material world which results in feeling the presence of some energy. Presentational learning refers to ways in which we communicate to others what we know; and propositional learning alludes to intellectual, logical, evidence-based reasoning. Practical learning is acquiring specific information and skills. Another consideration is that educators should consider learners' modalities of learning.

The first modality is *embodied sensation and feelings.* This is where the person first experiences a new feeling and sensation. These sensations may come in the form of a narrative, metaphor, image, physical, or material symbol. The second modality is *making sense of the new sensation.* This is where the learner experiences personal change referred to as transformative. The third modality is referred to as *conceptual analysis.* Here the learner starts to critique their worldview, use logical rational, and body knowledge (sensations in the body) that lead to transformative knowing and ultimately to reflective action (also referred to as *praxis*). Generally, the cycle begins with the learner encountering a new experience and having a cognitive and a *felt experience*. The learner is familiar with the felt sensation intuitively, hence it makes sense for them. In other situations, the experience arouses new sensations. Either way the learner extends the learning to a practical action. The practical action creates a new experience of felt encounter and the cycle continues. Considering that learners bring cognition, emotions, feelings, and spirit into the learning setting, educators require a framework and practical roadmap. The following consideration is provided: learners learn in relationship with others. This is to say that learners bring diverse or potentially divisive lived experiences to the learning setting. Thereby, practitioners should consider using images, storytelling, drawing, and other forms of expressions to combine cognitive and affective ways of knowing. Once learners experience other ways of knowing, there is a potential that workers build empathy toward others.

Embodiment

A word can have multiple meanings and depends on the context; the word *embodiment* is conceptualized in various ways. Embodiment is often referred to by other names, such as intuition, embodied consciousness, and embodied knowing. I use the term embodiment to mean cognitive and non-cognitive ways of knowing such as emotions, sensations, and feelings. I prefer to move away from binary thinking. For example, mind and body are integrated. In the context of anti-harassment training, a participant reported feeling activated. In other words, certain words and images invoked strong emotions, feelings, and sensations. The role of the facilitator is to invite participants to reflect and investigate the meaning of the bodily sensations and dig deeper to understand the root cause of the emotions, feelings, and sensations. Learning is more likely to be transformative if educators include the whole self rather than learning being confined to a rational cognitive realm.

Embodied learning is not a new phenomenon, but rather the most primitive ways of knowing. Human beings are born with an innate ability to learn through the body. However, in Western culture embodied learning is de-emphasized, and in my experience, the education system is often geared towards cognitive and rational models that negate alternative ways of knowing. For example, children in school are expected to sit in their chairs with little movement. I have observed this pattern replicated in higher education where students learn facts and figures in which there is a limited view of cognitive knowledge, and alternative ways of learning are discounted.

It is worth noting there are different ways of knowing: cognitive, affective, and spiritual, and all have physical components; hence, knowledge is embodied. A thought may invoke an emotion, and the emotion is likely to be carried in the body. Take for instance a person experiencing fear who may report discomfort in the abdomen and a person experiencing sadness reporting heaviness in the shoulders. Both narratives bear testimony that the body has wisdom and emotions are felt by the body. Hence, transformative learning is embodied learning. Reflexivity is a key element in transformative learning, and reflexivity engages emotions, thought, and somatic elements; hence, transformation learning is embodied.

Humans rely on a broad spectrum of gaining knowledge and being in the world (cognition, body, emotions, and spirit). Educators must consider using cognitive and non-cognitive activities in the classroom. One way that educators can incorporate embodied learning is by paying attention to non-verbal cues and facilitating experiential learning activities. For example, using physical movements, role play, storytelling, metaphor and images engages kinesthetics, thought and emotions, thereby engaging the whole person. That is to say the physical movements guide the person to deeper knowledge and when the body moves, the body thinks, and the mind incorporates the information in the reciprocal relationship. Educators who desire to invoke embodied learning must be made aware that learners bring different knowledge, experiences, identities, and cultures to the classroom. In oral cultures, for example, knowledge is shared in the body; hence, it requires deep listening on the part of the facilitator. Facilitators have to be aware that some learners rely on intuition, feeling, emotions, and spirit to guide their work and others focus strictly on head learning. Educators have to be cautious in introducing embodied learning as some learners may resist the idea of talking about emotions, feelings, and sensations in the body. The educator has to adjust their teaching approach to the diverse learning needs and provide coaching when required.

Humans rely on a broad spectrum of epistemology (cognition, body, emotions, and spirit) but epistemologies (how we know what we know) are relational, connected, and interconnected with nature, which means humans share knowledge with all creation. Humankind is not the only entity that has access to body knowledge: the cosmos, earth, nature, and animals also embody knowledge in a unique way.

How Educators Learn Embodied Learning

First and foremost, educators / facilitators need to be aware that we all learn differently. Physical, emotional, and spiritual components are also involved in learning beside head learning. Therefore, educators / facilitators should adopt models and techniques where we use different modalities to stimulate the involvement of students / participants and consequently improve the learning process as a whole. Starting with Rene Descartes in the seventeenth century, physical dimensions have long been overshadowed by cognitive sciences. The fact that body and mind are perceived as separate entities has deeply influenced the education system in the West. Therefore, learning experience is perceived as purely mental process, implemented through mental process such as reading, listening, and repeating the same information. Educators / facilitators need to learn about embodied learning and bring bodies back in the classroom and their teaching approach. Because we cannot learn without our bodies and we are not cognition on a stick, educators / facilitators need to focus on non-mental factors and incorporate physical movements, dance, poetry, art, games, role play, and acting, to name a few.

The Study Findings

The study (my doctorate dissertation) explored employees' perceptions of a mandatory anti-harassment training session and considered the potential of embodiment as a transformative pedagogical approach for anti-harassment training.

There is a lack of research regarding effectiveness of anti-harassment training, and in particular research that includes perceptions of employees. My research is timely because of several high-profile cases of workplace harassment that propelled a strong desire for training to address the problem. In addition, there is a statute of limitation on workplace harassment in

Canada because complaints must be made within 6 months up to 1 year in Canada after the alleged incident, which adds to the importance of anti-harassment training design.

Drawing on my doctorate dissertation, it is worth mentioning the nature of study and findings. I selected an organization that I referred as *The Firm*, a hierarchical, unionized, and public institution with over 13,000 employees. The Firm has an anti-harassment policy that states that their workforce includes people from different backgrounds, identities, needs, and perspectives; hence, creating and maintaining a work environment that is fully inclusive and respectful is essential.

Creating a respectful workplace is a shared responsibility of all employees. The anti-harassment policy clarifies roles and responsibilities and educates employees of their rights to work in a respectful work environment, free of harassment and discrimination. The anti-harassment policy also provides definitions and references to relevant policies and legislation. However, the anti-harassment policy does not provide guidelines for training; albeit the policy emphasizes that supervisors and managers have a responsibility to support and implement training and awareness. The anti-harassment curriculum includes legal definitions, case studies, complaint resolution processes, and resources for employees.

After I identified a local government organization that offered mandatory anti-harassment training to all staff, I selected employees who no longer worked for the organization. Selecting ex-employees was strategic, as many employees are afraid to speak up, in fear of reprisal. Four participants talked about their experiences outside of the anti-harassment training. Undoubtedly, their negative experiences might have impacted the responses; however, I did not inquire further. I used a referral system to recruit additional participants. I emailed one person I knew through a personal relationship and requested that they call me at their convenience. I spoke with the individuals on the phone and explained the scope of the study. Once I built rapport, I asked if they could refer me to other employees who no longer worked for The Firm and who would be willing to participate in the study. The telephone call was followed by an email where I thanked them for taking the time to speak with me on the phone and the letter of introduction. I contacted 11 participants in total and replicated a similar process. I felt that email was not sufficient, as I wanted to make a connection with the participants and hear their voices to gauge if they agreed or were hesitant to participate, as written text might not capture a participant's intention. Again, I wanted to get out of my head and get in touch with the body sensations.

Anytime I detected a bit of hesitation (long silences or a big sigh), I paused and gently reminded the individual that they were under no obligation to participate in the study. I received five emails from individuals suggesting they were unable to participate in the study. The refusal to participate in the study included: a lack of time, the nature of the topic, and refusal to re-live the trauma. Eventually, I recruited and interviewed six participants who attended an anti-harassment training in one locale. Participants voluntarily agreed and consented to participate in the study. I asked semi-structured questions, recorded, and transcribed the interviews. Each participant reviewed the transcript and adjusted as needed. I read the transcript as a whole document and read each transcript separately, then re-read the entire transcript. I used coding and identified key themes.

Four major themes emerged from the thematic analysis of the interview transcripts. The four major themes included: (a) closed and mechanical learning environment; (b) presence of body in learning; (c) bodily connection to mind, emotions, and spirit; and (d) the interaction of the head, heart, emotions, and spirit in decision-making. I interpreted participants' narratives to mean the anti-harassment training session was a closed and mechanical process, that the learning felt restrictive, and that the facilitator did not acknowledge the presence of the body in learning. Five participants felt apprehensive, overwhelmed, and unwelcome. Three participants perceived the classroom set-up as a barrier. There was a lack of flexibility in course design and information overload and a lack of welcoming protocols such as introductions and refreshments. There was a lack of trust in the classroom, and there were few classroom activities. Although the facilitators shared terms and concepts, it was evident that they overlooked diverse learning styles, epistemologies, and employees' social identity. The educational approach was didactic, which is traditionally teacher-centered. The focus was an information-giving approach. Participants brought their whole self into training (mind, body, emotions, and spirit), but the training design overlooked emotions, spirit, and body knowledge. The findings confirm that employees learn in a myriad of ways. This suggests that there is considerable potential for design improvement by incorporating the whole person approach where the information moves from the head to the heart.

The study generated new understandings about anti-harassment training, starting with the learning environment and teaching approach in facilitating anti-harassment training. All six participants attended a compulsory, structured, formal anti-harassment training session in a traditional classroom led by a facilitator. The participants struggled in the classroom due to the inflexibility in program design. The anti-harassment training design did not allow for different learning styles or critical reflection with self and others. Participants acknowledged embodied knowing, yet the anti-harassment program design did not allow for the whole person learning. The participants highlighted the importance of the social identity of the trainer and employees. The facilitator has to be familiar with the whole person teaching approach before they can teach the whole person. The anti-harassment training did not meet the learning needs of employees, and the learning environment did not afford the whole person model. The findings are significant because they may contribute to an effective anti-harassment training, and these elements need to be factored into anti-harassment course design.

Even though the impact of the physical environment on learning is well-documented in adult education, the importance of the physical setting and learning environment lack mention in the literature on anti-harassment training. The AHRC provides guidelines to employers in creating an anti-harassment policy, however, there are no guidelines on anti-harassment training for employers. Although there is minimal research evidence of the importance of learning environments in relation to anti-harassment training, the interviews with the six participants clearly indicate that employees desired a welcoming learning space, the removal of tables and chairs, engagement, and interactions with other participants, embodied knowing factored into the program design, and building rapport with the facilitator. These findings not only contribute to understanding the architecture of the learning space but also to the importance of the program design and learning environment.

Workplace training in general must move beyond a cognitive-rational approach towards a whole person model, which proposes the incorporation of a range of techniques to engage the whole person in learning. The existing literature demonstrates that adult education is not merely a mechanical activity and that educators need to pay attention to the social context of learning and learning that goes beyond cognitive processes. This is inarguably the case with anti-harassment training in the workplace. Anti-harassment training has to incorporate the body, mind, emotions, and spirituality toward whole person transformative learning. Hence, workplace educators should incorporate embodied learning into anti-harassment program design. Despite considerable shifts in workplace training since the Industrial Revolution, facilitators will continue to play in integral role in training workers. There is a considerable body of research to understand the influence of the facilitator and facilitation characteristics on participants, in general theory, and the facilitator's core role, responsibilities, and function. However, there is no single study that explores the facilitator's role in an anti-harassment training in North America and Europe.

Recommendations for Practitioners, Trainers, and HR Policy Makers

Five lessons emerged from this research.

First and foremost, Canada needs a centralized entity, ideally the Canadian Human Rights Commission (CHRC), to collect and aggregate data on harassment in the workplace.

Second, the CHRC should develop a standard policy for anti-harassment training and track anti-harassment program effectiveness. The EEOC in the United States is a viable reference. The EEOC suggests that training should be a minimum of 4 hours, live, interactive, include case studies, role play, and should allow participants to have an opportunity to ask questions.

Although the EEOC's recommendations are remarkable by providing clear guidelines on anti-harassment training, training remains rooted in cognitive and rational models. Essentially, anti-harassment training must move beyond passive approaches (PowerPoint and lecture), mere compliance, and a check box. The whole person approach discourages disembodied thinking—mind-body dualism—and values whole person learning.

Third, anti-harassment training cannot be separated from the workplace context. Transformative learning and the whole person approach is a major shift from traditional anti-harassment training. Hence, HR practitioners and trainers need to be creative in how they get buy-in from senior leaders in the organization and manage resistance and backlash from employers and trainees.

Fourth, HR practitioners and trainers need to fully embrace and embody the whole person approach and ensure the program objectives, design, and evaluation are aligned.

Finally, it is important that trainers carefully track whether or not the whole person approach in teaching anti-harassment programs reduces workplace harassment. Anti-harassment training is seen as a panacea for all the problems; however, such programs are also not always evaluated for their effectiveness and long-term impact.

Process for Incorporating the Whole Person Approach to Anti-harassment Training

Despite these limitations, there are some wise practices worth incorporating into anti-harassment training. These guidelines are rooted in the literature, theoretical framework, and data analysis.

- Anti-harassment training should be 4 hours or longer in length, should be facilitated by an adult education specialist and an SME, who together can embrace and embody the whole person approach in teaching the anti-harassment workshop.

- Training is best conducted in a designated training room, or a classroom removed from the worksite for privacy and in a space where the employees feel comfortable sharing information about workplace harassment.

- Facilitators play an integral role in creating a supportive and inclusive learning environment. Hence, the facilitators should conduct a needs assessment prior to the start of the anti-harassment workshop to gauge learning styles and range of understanding about workplace harassment.

- Content can be tailored to meet the diverse learning styles and array of understanding.

- Facilitators should greet trainees upon arrival and be directed to sit in a circle.

- Circles are an effective way to start the training by inviting trainees to share their feelings and listen to others. The facilitator should include themselves in the circle to signal that they are facilitators and listeners during training, not authority figures. Sitting in a circle and sharing thoughts and feelings could potentially lead to building trusting relationship with trainees.

- Everyone in the circle should have an opportunity to introduce themselves and share their thoughts and embodied experiences pertaining to anti-harassment training. The group activities should be inclusive and interactive. Interactive activities will help build relationships with other participants.

- It is also ideal to have light refreshments for trainees.

- The facilitator should invite all participants to develop training rules of engagement. Facilitators should inquire about trainees' social identity and learning styles during class. This is to ensure that everyone in the training is aware of diverse learning modalities.

- The facilitator should share the course objectives but remain flexible to accommodate trainees' questions and concerns. Training should build on trainees' experiences.

- Course content should have relevance to and impact on their job and personal life.

- The teaching approach should remain respectful, dialogical, and learner centered.

- There should be an opportunity for consciousness raising, critical self-reflection, and empowerment.

- The facilitator may or may not use a PowerPoint but should incorporate different learning modalities such as storytelling, journal writing, video, documentary film, art, role play, drama, and dance. The facilitator should be self-aware of their biases and vigilant about triggers and backlash. Facilitators have to acknowledge that both mind and body are engaged in learning; hence they need to embody the whole person model and feel comfortable in teaching the whole person.

CONCLUSION

According to the Alberta Human Rights Commission (AHRC), workplace harassment is defined as a single or repeated incident of objectionable or unwelcome conduct, comment, bullying or action intended to intimidate, offend, degrade or humiliate a particular person or group. Behind every anti-harassment complaint, are individuals who suffer a loss of dignity, contentment, and productivity and may miss or forego job advancement opportunities. The consequences of such behaviour for individuals and organizations are dire.

Organizations should develop a robust anti-harassment policy that fosters an environment of respect for human rights and helps people in the organization understand their rights and responsibilities. The policy should be accompanied by anti-harassment training. Contemporary anti-harassment training design is ineffective as it relies on pushing the information out rather than understanding participants' experiences with workplace bullying and invoking the policy. The anti-harassment training cannot rely solely on legal definition but rather it should use real scenarios in the workplace to enforce the policy. Facilitators cannot solely rely on PowerPoint presentations, on-line, and one-way communication. Training should be a minimum of 4 hours and to be effective it has to be interactive. During the pandemic when many of us have been forced to teach online, facilitators must make every effort to connect with the learners as individuals, create a psychologically safe place to learn, and welcome learners' input. Anti-harassment training needs to be rooted in a constructive dialogue, real case studies, and role plays where applicable. If the training is conducted live, there should be physical movement.

There is no national data bank in Canada that tracks incidents of bullying, harassment, and discrimination complaints in the workplace. Until such data is available, every organization needs a baseline to determine if training makes a difference in reducing workplace harassment. Training alone is insufficient. However, anti-harassment training is ubiquitous, yet incidents of harassment continue to be reported; hence, practitioners need to scrutinize contemporary anti-harassment programs and consider characteristics of the learners and workplace context when designing a program for their organization. Program designers and facilitators should ask questions about their current program such as, how does anti-harassment training impact those in positions of power and those in the margins? And perhaps most importantly facilitators need to feel comfortable interrogating their own identity and how their views and experiences impact their work. Anti-harassment training must build on the learner / worker's experience, include critical dialogue, self-reflection, and whole person learning.

APPENDIX

Anti-harassment training is rooted in the company's anti-harassment policy. The purpose of anti-harassment policy is to provide clear guidelines on what constitutes harassment, how employees can report an incident, as well as procedures to resolve complaints.

The purpose of anti-harassment training is to ensure that employees are aware of the company's policy and ways in which their behaviours could constitute harassment as defined in the company's policy. Employees should come away from the training with a clear understanding of behaviour that could potentially impact another employee. The aim should be a fundamental shift in behaviors and attitudes; thereby reducing workplace harassment.

For learners / workers to make such a shift, they need the necessary skills to identify workplace harassment. Individuals who experience harassment need to know how to resolve conflicts, when to involve a supervisor, and other authority when needed.

Organizations vary in size and though many have similar physical workplaces, each of them is unique and develop their own culture. Therefore, it is difficult to produce a comprehensive checklist for an anti-harassment program that will work for every single organization. However, there are wise best practices to consider when developing individual training programs. These are rooted in the literature and my personal experience.

Trainer

It is imperative that trainers or facilitators hosting the anti-harassment training spend significant time reflecting on their social location, positionality, and intersectionality. An individual's social location is defined as the combination of factors including gender, race, social class, age, ability, religion, sexual orientation, and geographic location. Positionality refers to the how differences in social position and power shape identities and determine access in society. Intersectionality is the acknowledgment that everyone has their own unique experiences of discrimination and oppression, and we must consider everything and anything that can marginalize people–gender, race, class, sexual orientation, and physical ability, to name a few.

If for instance, when a facilitator is not familiar with or able to relate to microinequities, microaggressions, and racism because they have not experienced it firsthand, there is a higher risk of minimizing or dismissing someone's experience. By acknowledging their lack of knowledge but aware of the importance of such experiences, they will be better able to address and recognize the variable experience of workers and learners.

Facilitators should be open and vulnerable by sharing their social location and inviting participants to do the same. This way facilitators model bringing their whole selves to the anti-harassment training and encourage participants to do the same.

Preparation

The training content depends on training objectives. Facilitators want to ensure that anti-harassment training is offered to both employees and managers. Facilitators should determine some of the characteristics of the participants. It is helpful to know their name, ranks, length of service, and level of literacy regarding workplace harassment. An on-line pre-workshop survey can be attached to the training invite. It is important to check what information facilitators are allowed to request under both company policy and without violating human rights. If collecting the information on paper is not a possibility, the facilitator can always build in activities that explores participant's social location, positionality, and intersectionality. Literacy levels can also be assessed during in class activities.

Space and Time

While it is ideal to host the training live and in person with a minimum of 4 hours, it is not always possible. The recent pandemic for instance forced workplaces to become virtual and interpersonal relations between employees were restricted. This situation would have impacted any training programs in the organization. When conducting a live session, it is ideal to have no more than 25 participants. For online training, I suggest a maximum of 15 participants. I have had the most success hosting live sessions outside of the workplace. A change of location often gets participants to expand their thinking and they do not feel compelled to respond to work demands. It is imperative to have an open space for training where participants can move around and do not feel crammed.

Facilitators need to set the date and time for training sessions. Try to keep the schedule consistent, for example the training will take place every week on a Wednesday at 9:00 am. This makes it easy for employees to attend by being able to book the time into their work week.

Accessibility

Ensure the physical space is inclusive if training is conducted live and in person. The space has to accommodate differently abled participants. If possible, get an American Sign Language (ASL) interpreter if there are attendees who may be deaf or hard of hearing. If the training is conducted online, ensure that everyone has access to a computer, a reliable network, and ensure that closed captions are turned on to ensure that all participants can hear and see the presentation.

Method

Do not rely solely on the PowerPoint presentation to host a dialogue. If the meeting is in person, ensure that you walk around, make eye contact with each participant, and assign them to a table. This is to ensure that groups who work together do not form their own niche and ignore the other participants. If training online, ensure there are three to five breakout sessions.

Training Design

Introduction

Arrive early, ensure that all equipment is working. If the meeting is online, ensure that all participants have clear guidelines as to how to get connected (i.e., Zoom, Google Meet, etc.) and ensure the link is working and accessible to participants with different abilities.

First and foremost, make a connection with all the participants. Welcome them to the workshop. Whether training is conducted in person or online, ensure that all participants display their preferred name and pronouns. Create a safe learning environment where everyone respects each other.

Introduce yourself and ask others to do the same. Begin with a brief icebreaker or a poll asking participants questions such as if they are a pet owner, if they have a hobby, or a favorite holiday destination. The introduction and ice-breaker initiates conversations between participants, therefore it is imperative that a trainer allow time for participants to interact with each other. Interacting with each other has a potential to build trust.

Define the Process

After the introduction, it is always a wise idea to set terms of relationship in consultation with the participants.

Speak: Speak from our own experiences and perspectives.

Listen: Listen generously to the experiences and perspectives of others, create supportive space for each person to learn.

Do not interrupt when others are speaking.

Allow space for introverts and individuals who require time to reflect.

Resist: Actively resist making assumptions about one another.

Refrain: Refrain from fixing, saving, advising, or correcting each other

Be: mindful of *taking space and making space* to ensure everyone has opportunities to speak and to listen

Respect: Respect the confidentiality of personal information and stories shared here.

Facilitators should be mindful as to how they show up. This is to say, if you want participants to be respectful, then they should model appropriate behaviour such as staying calm, using correct pronouns, inclusive language, and debriefing with participants when things do not go as planned.

After the learners understand the terms of relationship, the facilitator should introduce a social location, positionality, and intersectionality exercise. This exercise should alert participants that diversity is the norm, and everyone has unique identities, privileges, and disadvantages (see Figure 1).

For this exercise the participants are asked to identify their social class, age, gender, sexual identity, race, other identifiers and the next step is to highlight some of the advantages they have. Below I have provided my own example:

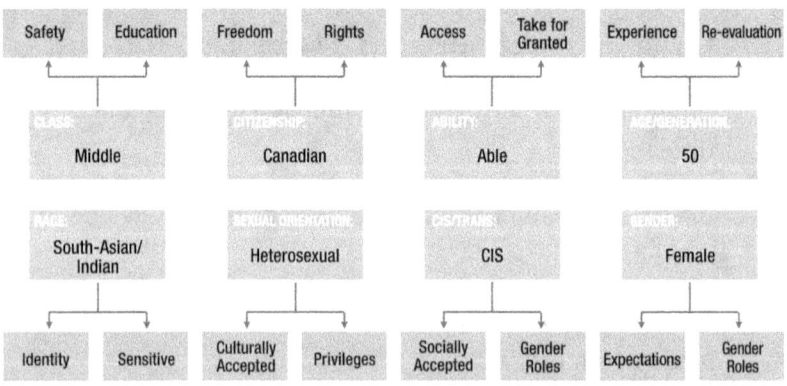

Figure 1: Social Location and Intersectionality

Appendix

Before introducing the legislation and company's complaint resolution processes, start by asking participants their understanding of workplace harassment. Ask participants to share their experience(s) regarding conflict in the workplace. Facilitators can introduce case studies, vignettes, videos, and images after listening to the participants. Promote whole person learning. Invite participants to think and feel. I often ask participants to pay attention to how they feel when I introduce a topic. I inquire if they feel energized or drained. Do they notice any physiological changes? A rapid heart rate, anxiety, knots in the stomach. If yes, I create a safe space for participants to interrogate the feelings. Participants need space to explore their emotions. Do they feel angry, hurt, or helpless? Together as a group, we talk through the thinking, feeling, and being.

Anti-harassment work could potentially introduce a trigger for some of the participants, therefore it is essential the facilitators are aware of trauma informed teaching practices. While there are many definitions of trauma, I rely on the work of Dr. Mate Gabor (see references and further reading). Trauma is the lasting emotional response that often results from living through a distressing event. Trauma could be severe physical abuse, neglect, death of a loved one, or collective trauma. It is wise to refer participants to a company sponsored EAP (Employee Assistance Program) or an external counselor of their choice at the start of the anti-harassment training. It is important to note that trauma resides in the mind and body; hence facilitators should allow for the whole person learning.

Role play exercises give participants the opportunity to assume the role of a person or act out a given situation. These roles can be performed by individual participants in pairs or in groups which can play out a more complex scenario. Role plays engage participants in real-life workplace situations or scenarios that can be stressful, unfamiliar, complex, or controversial which requires them to examine personal feelings toward others and their circumstances

Role play exercises are usually short, spontaneous presentations but also can be prearranged before the start of the workshop. Role play often enhances learning because of providing real-world scenarios to help participants learn. Role play also provides opportunities for critical observations of peers. For example, a workplace bullying scenario could be role played by two participants and other participants are invited to consider *how would you manage this situation*.

Be careful with role plays as that could potentially trigger participants the wrong way. Therefore, it is important to set guidelines. If planning to use role playing, start with some simple scenarios such as a micro-inequity (not introducing someone, mispronouncing someone's name repeatedly) before sharing a complex discrimination scenario. Will participants have an opportunity to debrief after the role play? I find it helpful to have participants comment on what they have observed followed by a revised version of how to handle workplace harassment. This way participants are taught how to properly assess what constitute harassment and ways to mitigate the situation. Tie role plays to learning objectives, so students see their relevance to course content.

Training

After the introduction, ensure that participants work in pairs or groups. This ensures that everyone feels their voice matters and they feel included, but it also builds a community of practice i.e., someone in the group offers a tip or advice that helped them navigate conflict in the workplace.

Set ground rules for the breakout session. Ensure that everyone gets an opportunity to speak and share their experiences. Participants also have the option to pass if they choose. Allow sufficient time for the breakout session to ensure that everyone gets a chance to share.

Accommodate different learning styles. Some learners are auditory, others are visual and kinesthetics. It is always a good idea to have participants physically move around the room and post their ideas on the wall; however, the physical movement is not conducive to on-line learning. Facilitators can still share information using different methods such as written / text, audio, and videos. Ensure to gauge participants' experience in attending the anti-harassment training and suggestions for improvements. I don't want to be overly prescriptive, however, the goal of any training is to connect, introduce the topic, have participants reflect, and try out the activities and debrief.

After Training

Employers should require employees and managers to sign a statement confirming that they have attended the training and understood what they have been told. This can be used as documentation, which the employer can point to as a way to show their commitment to a harassment-free workplace.

Conduct a 3-month follow-up of 20% of the participants every quarter to gauge transfer of knowledge and barriers to implementing the policy.

FINAL WORD

Undoubtedly, practitioners need to consider improving anti-harassment effectiveness. However, there is scant research on the type of training that will guarantee a reduction of complaints and litigation costs. There is ample research suggesting wise practices. For example, in 2018, the Society of Human Resources Management (SHRM) surveyed 1078 organization and 32% indicated they had amended sexual harassment prevention program. The changes included adding a workplace civility component, customized training, training for new on boards / hires. Another 22% indicated they will make changes, and some have added by-standard training. However, the companies who made the changes to the program did not report on program effectiveness.

We certainly need strong anti-harassment legislation, interactive training, bi-annual refreshers, a separate training for supervisors highlighting core responsibilities, and training that includes actual case studies, and scenarios. We also need to mention incivility in training, offer a variety of modalities such as blended training, and make training interactive and conversational. Despite significant gains, both academics and practitioners do not provide concrete steps to ensure a reduction of workplace harassment. Therefore, it is equally difficult to make absolute claims that a particular design will guarantee a reduction in harassment complaints and litigation costs (on the contrary the number of complaints may potentially rise as employees become aware of the process). On the other hand, an ineffective training may exacerbate the problem further.

Outcome Based Approach: Moving Beyond Attendance

Anytime we design and deliver the anti-harassment training we want to know how effective it is. This is to say is training making a difference for the individual, and wider organization. I am drawing on Kirkpatrick's training evaluation model as one way to analyze training effectiveness. The model has four successive levels that measure effectiveness of a training program: reaction, learning, behaviour, and results.

Level I: reaction captures participant's satisfaction level with training. In other words, was training valuable, engaging, was the instructor respectful and addressed different learning styles.

Level II: focuses on measuring if training helped participant increase their knowledge of workplace harassment, complaint resolution process and ways to mitigate conflict. Facilitators want to gauge what participants will do different because of training, how confident they feel, and if they are motivated to change their behaviours.

Level III: is concerned with behaviours. Behaviour captures transfer of knowledge. In other works, can participants apply learning after the training session. It is plausible that learners increased their knowledge during training; however, they were unable to use the knowledge because the workplace conditions were not favourable. One way to gauge transfer of knowledge is conducting interviews or sending participants an online survey after training is completed. In the ideal situation, organizations would collect the data from the interviews, identify gaps in transfer of knowledge, and provide coaching and other supports. The following vignette showcase one such study I conducted in 2010.

Vignette

The corporate Respectful Workplace (RWP) Training is a 3-hour comprehensive mandatory training session designed to ensure every employee is fully versed in the Respectful Workplace. The primary goal is to ensure that staff can contribute to a highly respectful work environment free from harassment and discrimination. This goal is increasingly an imperative, as the company attempts to attract and retain a diverse workforce within an increasingly competitive global labour market.

Training Design and Evaluation

To continuously gauge and improve training outcomes, all participants complete an in-class post-session evaluation form. Results of the in-class evaluations was aggregated and provided to senior leaders in the corporation. That results indicated a 92% satisfaction rate. Evaluation of training outcomes following trainees' return to the workplace is often viewed as a more meaningful gauge of the outcomes of adult education. A telephone follow-up survey of 20% of participants has been conducted by a researcher a minimum of 3 months after RWP training participation.

The results included that 574 employees completed RWP training, and a total 114 employees participated in the telephone evaluation survey. No members of the sample declined the opportunity to contribute their perspectives. RWP training evaluation respondents were randomly selected from the complete list of RWP trainees. Respondents were informed that the survey is confidential and that their responses would be grouped to ensure anonymity. Respondents were also informed that demographic data will be collected for statistical purposes only.

Findings

- 81% of respondents agree that they are more aware of barriers to inclusion (65% agree, 16% strongly agree).

- 87% of respondents agree that they have an improved understanding of their role in creating an inclusive workplace (60% agree, 27% strongly agree.)

- 73% of respondents agree that they have an improved ability to recognize their own biases (55% agree, 18% strongly agree).

- 82% of respondents agree that they have increased confidence in their ability to address inclusion issues they may face (67% agree, 15% strongly agree).

- 78% of respondents agree that they feel supported in addressing inclusion barriers (62% agree, 16% strongly agree).

Respondents also identified barriers to inclusion that they are experiencing in their workplace:

1. Lack of colleagues' understanding of diversity beyond *cultural* diversity

2. Gender bias

3. Lack of respect for one another

4. Structural barriers such as hiring processes.

Respondents indicated their attempts to address these barriers have included:

1. Self-education

2. Bringing barriers to the attention of their supervisors

3. Improvement of hiring practices.

Other ideas respondents had about how barriers could be addressed on a corporate wide basis included the following themes:

1. Provision of more targeted training, for example intercultural training

2. Development and implementation of more specific corporate-wide strategies to support implementation of Respectful Workplace and related directives

3. Bringing of barriers to the attention of supervisors.

Some additional themes that emerged from respondents' evaluations included:

1. The desirability of earlier-and regular-evaluation follow-ups on the outcomes of training

2. The need for personal accountability on the part of those in leadership and supervisory positions

3. The need for examination of the root causes of workplace disrespect issues.

This vignette is shared to highlight the significance of post workshop evaluation as it digs deeper into the challenges of transfer of knowledge.

Level IV: Results are probably most costly and time consuming. Therefore, it is imperative to establish a baseline for various aspects including participant's attitudes, confidence, commitment, number of harassment complaints, litigation costs, employee engagement, workplace culture, turnover, and reputation, to name a few.

All this is to say is that practitioners should determine participant's skills, knowledge, attitudes, and motivation before and after training. Depending on the size of the company, the first year the anti-harassment training is introduced, and employees become aware of legislation and complaint resolution process. There will potentially be a rise in complaints. Program administrators can certainly obtain reactions to training post training; gauging transfer of knowledge requires a deeper dive, such as an online or telephone survey. Year 2 or 3 is when one might notice complaints start to plateau. Employees have the skills to resolve interpersonal conflicts, formal complaints are investigated, workplace restoration is implemented, and businesses and organization achieve their strategic goals.

BIBLIOGRAPHY

Albert Human Rights Commission (AHRC). (2019). *Roles and responsibilities for employer.* https://www.albertahumanrights.ab.ca/education/Pages/e_learning.aspx

Alberta Human Rights Commission. (2019). *Annual report.* https://www.albertahumanrights.ab.ca/Documents/AHRC_Annual_Report_2017_18.pdf

Alberta Occupational Health, and Safety Code. (2019). http://www.qp.alberta.ca/documents/OHS/OHSCode.pdf

Anand, R., & Winters, M. (2008). A retrospective view of corporate diversity training from 1964 to the present. *Academy of Management Learning & Education, 7*, 356-372.

Anderson, L. M., & Pearson, C. M. (1999). Tit for tat?: The spiraling effect of incivility in the workplace. *The Academy of Management Review, 24*(3), 452-471.

Antecol, H., & Cobb-Clark, D. (2003). Does sexual harassment training change attitudes?: A view from the federal level. *Social Science Quarterly, 84*(4), 826-842.

Arnold, A. (2018, May 30). *4 Starbucks employees on what the racial-bias training was really like.* https://www.thecut.com/2018/05/starbucks-employees-racial-bias-training.html

Austin, I., & Porter, C. (2018, January 23). *In Canada, A 'perfect storm' for a #MeToo reckoning.* https://www.nytimes.com/2018/01/29/world/canada/metoo-sexualharassment.html?

Bainbridge, H. T. J., Perry, E. L., & Kulik, C. T. (2018). Sexual harassment training: Explaining differences in Australian and US approaches. *Asia Pacific Journal of Human Resources, 56*, 124-147.

Balm, J. E. (2005). *The perceived influence of some trainee characteristics and conditions for transfer on training outcomes.* https://ro.ecu.edu.au/theses/622

Bartlett, E. J., & Bartlett, E. M. (2011). Workplace bullying: An integrative literature review. *Advances in Developing Human Resources, 13*(1), 69-84.

Baumgartner, L. (2001). An update on transformational learning. *New Directions for Adult and Continuing Education, 89*, 15-24.

Belch, D. (2018, May 22). *Employee "training" in corporate America doesn't work. Here's why.* The Medium. https://medium.com/@STRIVR/employee-training-in-corporate-america-doesnt-work-here-s-why-497739f05e0e

Bingham, S. G., & Scherer, L. L. (2001). The unexpected effects of a sexual harassment educational program. *The Journal of Applied Behavioral Science, 37*(2), 125-153.

Bissell-Linsk, J., Dye, J., & Nicolaou, A. (2018, April 17). *Starbucks to close all US stores for racial bias training.* https://www.ft.com/content/8c3d4096-4274-11e8-803a-295c97e6fd0b

Bisom-Rapp, S. (2018). Sex harassment training must change: The case for legal incentives for transformative education and prevention. *Stanford Law Review, 71*, 60-73.

Boud, D., & Garrick, J. (1999). *Understanding learning at work.* Routledge.

Boyd, R. D., & Myers J. G. (1988). Transformative education. *International Journal of Lifelong Education, 7*(4), 261-284.

Brown, A., & Kuzz, E. R. (2016). *Bullying and harassment: In Canada it is no longer just a school yard issue.* https://www.sherrardkuzz.com/pdf/kuzz_iba_oct_bullying.pdf

Buchanan, N. T., Settles, I. H., Hall, A. T., & O'Connor, R. C. (2014). A review of organizational strategies for reducing sexual harassment: Insights from the U.S. military. *Journal of Social Issues, 70*(4), 687-702.

Burke, L. A., & Hutchins, H. M. (2007). Training transfer: An integrative literature review. *Human Resource Development Review, 6*(3), 263-296.

Campo, C. (2017, October 26). *The Weinstein ripple effect: Famous men accused of sexual harassment and assault.* https://www.cnbc.com/2017/10/26/the-weinstein-ripple-effect-famous-men-accused-of-sexual-harassment-and-assault.html

BIBLIOGRAPHY

Canadian Human Rights Commission (CHRC). (2019). *Annual report.* http://chrcreport.ca/assets/pdf/CHRC_AR_2018-ENG.pdf

Carlsen, A., Salam, M., Miller, C. C., Lu, D., Ngu, A., Patel, J. K., & Wichter, Z. (2018, October 29). *#MeToo brought down 201 powerful men. Nearly half of their replacements are women.* The New York Times. https://www.nytimes.com/interactive/2018/10/23/us/metoo-replacements.html

Chai, R. R. (2019). *Anti-harassment training in the era of #MeToo.* https://www.td.org/magazines/td-magazine/anti-harassment-training-in-the-era-of-metoo

Chappell, B. (2018, May 29). *Starbucks closes more than 8,000 stores today for racial bias training.* https://www.npr.org/sections/thetwo-way/2018/05/29/615119351/starbucks-closes-more-than-8-000-stores-today-for-racial-bias-training

Clement, D. (2013). Legacies and implications of human rights law in Canada. *Canadian Issues,* 46-50.

Clement, D., & Trottier, D. (2012). *The evolution of human rights in Canada.* Canadian Human Rights Commission.

Cortina, L. M., Magley, V. J., Williams, J. H., & Langhout, R. D. (2001). Incivility in the workplace: Incidence and impact. *Journal of Occupational Health Psychology, 6*(1), 64-80.

Cranton, P. (2016). *Understanding and promoting transformative learning: A guide to theory and practice* (3rd ed.). Stylus Publishing.

Crenshaw, K. (1991). Mapping the margins: Intersectionality, identity politics, and violence against women of color. *Stanford Law Review, 43*(6), 1241–1299.

Davenport, T. H. (2006). Competing on analytics. *Harvard Business Review, 84*(1), 98-107.

Davies, J. (2017). *Word cloud generator.* https://www.jasondavies.com/wordcloud/

Dalgarno, B., & Lee, M. J. (2010). What are the learning affordances of 3-D virtual environments? *British Journal of Educational Technology, 41*(1), 10-32.

Dewey, J. (1938). *Experience and education.* Macmillan.

Dirkx, J. M. (1998). Transformative learning theory in the practice of adult education: An overview. Pennsylvania Association for Adult Continuing Education (PAACE). *Journal of Lifelong Learning, 7,* 1-14.

Dirkx, J. M. (2000). *Transformative learning and the journey of individuation* (ERIC Digests No. 223; ED 448305). ERIC Clearing house on Adult, Career, & Vocational Education.

Dirkx, J. M. (2001). The power of feelings: Emotion, imagination, and the construction of meaning in adult learning. *New Directions for Adult and Continuing Education, 89,* 63-72.Dirkx, J. M. (2001a). Images, transformative learning, and the work of the soul. *Adult Learning, 12*(3), 15-16.

Dirkx, J. M. (2006). Engaging emotions in adult learning: A Jungian perspective on emotion and transformative learning. In E. W. Taylor (Ed.), *Teaching for change new directions for adult and continuing education* (pp. 15-26). Jossey-Bass.

Dirkx, J. M. (2008). The meaning and role of emotions in adult learning. *New Directions for Adult and Continuing Education, 120,* 7-18.

Dobbin, F., & Kalev, A. (2019). The promise and peril of sexual harassment programs. *Proceedings of the National Academy of Sciences, 116*(25), 12255-12260.

Eatough, E. M., Waters, S. D., & Kellerman, G. R. (2019). Evidence-based recommendations for improved design of sexual harassment training. *Industrial and Organizational Psychology: Perspectives on Science and Practice, 12*(1), 48-51.

Einarsen, S., Aasland, M. S., & Skogstad, A. (2007). Destructive leadership behavior: A definition and conceptual model. *The Leadership Quarterly, 18,* 207-216.

Einarsen, S., Hoel, H., Zapf, D., & Cooper, C. L. (2010). The concept of bullying at work: The European tradition. In S. Einarsen, H. Hoel, D. Zapf, & C. L. Cooper (Eds.), Bullying and emotional abuse in the workplace. *International Perspectives in Research and Practice* (pp. 3-30). Taylor & Francis.

Einarsen, S., Hoel, H., Zapf, D., & Cooper, C. (Eds.). (2010*). Bullying and harassment in the workplace. Developments in theory, research and practice* (2nd ed.). Taylor and Francis Group.

Ellstrom, P. (2011). Informal learning at work: Conditions, processes and logics. In M. Malloch L. Cairns & K. Evans *The SAGE handbook of workplace learning* (pp. 105-119).

Embodiment. (n.d.). In *Merriam-Webster.com dictionary*. https://www.merriam-webster.com/thesaurus/embodiment

Employment and Social Development Canada. (2017). *Harassment and sexual violence in the workplace*. https://www.canada.ca/en/employment-social-development/services/health-safety/reports/workplace-harassment-sexual-violence.html

Equal Employment Opportunity Commission (EEOC). (2019). *Promising practices for preventing harassment*. Washington, DC.

Feldblum, C., & Lipnic, V. (2016). Select task force on the study of harassment in the workplace. *Equal Employment Opportunity Commission (EEOC)*. https://www.eeoc.gov/eeoc/task_force/harassment/upload/report.pdf

Fernandez, A. C., Huang, J., & Rinaldo, V. (2011). Does where a student sits really matter? The impact on seating locations on student classroom learning. *International Journal of Applied Educational Studies*, *10*(1), 66–77.

Fletcher, C. (2018). Starbucks' training shutdown could cost it just US$16.7M https://www.bloomberg.com/news/articles/2018-04-17/starbucks-training-shutdown-could-cost-them-just-16-7-million

Fritz, J., & Whitman, J. (2017). Moving the heart *and* head: Implications for learning analytics research. https://er.educause.edu/articles/2017/7/moving-the-heart-and-head-implications-for-learning-analytics-research

Folz, C. (2016, June 19). No evidence that training prevents harassment, finds EEOC task force. *Society for Human Resource Management*. https://www.shrm.org/hr-today/news/hrnews/pages/eeoc-harassment-task-force.aspx

Freire, P. (1970/1996). *Pedagogy of the oppressed* (M. B. Ramos, Trans.). Penguin Books.

John, F., & Whitmer, J. (2017, February 27). *Moving the heart and head: Implications for learning analytics research*. Educause Review. https://er.educause.edu/articles/2017/7/moving-the-heart-and-head-implications-for-learning-analytics-research

Froyd, J., & Simpson, N. (2008). *Student-centered learning: Addressing faculty question about student-centered learning*, [Paper presentation]. Course, Curriculum, Labor, and Improvement Conference, Washington, DC. http://www.ccliconference.com/2008.../Froyd_StuCenteredLearning.pdf

Gupta, R., Gupta, A., & Nehra, D. (2019). Going forward with #MeToo movement: Towards a safer work environment. *Journal of Psychosexual Health*, *1*(2), 174-179.

Hango, D., & Moyser, M. (2018). *Harassment in Canadian workplace*. https://www150.statcan.gc.ca/n1/pub/75-006-x/2018001/article/54982-eng.pdf

Hassard, J. S. (2012). Rethinking the Hawthorne studies: The Western Electric research in its social, political, and historical context. *Human Relations*, *65*(11), 1431-1461.

Hastie, B. (2019). *Workplace sexual harassment: Assessing the effectiveness of human rights law in Canada*. University of British Columbia.

Heron, J. (1992). *Feeling and personhood: Psychology in another key*. Sage Publications.

Hershcovis, M. S., & Barling, J. (2010). Towards a multi-foci approach to workplace aggression: A meta-analytic review of outcomes from different perpetrators. *Journal of Organizational Behavior*, *31*, 24.

Immen, W. (2013, February 6). *Mobile workers are the 'new norm'*. The Globe and Mail. https://www.theglobeandmail.com/report-on-business/careers/the-future-of-work/mobile- workers-are-the-new-norm/article8295535/

Illeris, K. (2017). Peter Jarvis and the understanding of adult learning. *International Journal of Lifelong Education*, *36*(1-2), 35-44.

Itzchakov, G., & Kluger, A. N. (2017). Can holding a stick improve listening at work?: The effect of listening circles on employees' emotions and cognitions. *European Journal of Work and Organizational Psychology*, *26*(5), 663-676.

Kasl, E., & Yorks, L. (2002). Collaborative inquiry for adult learning. In L. Yorks & E. Kasl (Eds.), *Collaborative inquiry as a strategy for adult learning* (pp. 3-11). Jossey-Bass.

Kaplan, B., & Manchester, J (2018). *The power of vulnerability: How to create a team of leaders by shifting inwards*. Green Leaf Book.

Kerka, S. (2002). *Somatic/embodied learning and adult education*. http://www.calpro-online.org/eric/docs/tia00100

Kersh, N. (2015). Rethinking the learning space at work and beyond: The achievement of agency across the boundaries of work-related spaces and environments. *International Review of Education*, *61*(6), 835-851.

Lawrence, R. L., Nieves, Y., Snowber, C., Kong, L., & Ntseane, G. (2013). *Embodied knowing: Getting back to our roots.* http://newprairiepress.org/aerc/2013/symposia/2

Leatherman, D. (2007). *The training trilogy: Conducting needs assessments, designing programs, training Skills* (3rd ed.). HRD Press.

Magley, V. J., & Grossman, J. L. (2017, November 10). *Do sexual harassment prevention trainings really work?* [Blog post]. https://blogs.scientificamerican.com/observations/

Mate, G. (2003). *When the body says no: The cost of hidden stress.* Toronto: Knopf Canada.

Mate, G. (2009). *In the realm of hungry ghosts*: Close encounters with addiction. Toronto: Knopf Canada.

Mezirow, J. (1971). Toward a theory of practice. *Adult Education, 21*, 135-147.

Mezirow, J. (1978). Perspective transformation. *Adult Education, 28*, 100-110.

Mezirow, J. (1981). A critical theory of adult learning and education. *Adult Education, 32*, 3-24.

Mezirow, J. (2009). Transformative learning theory. In J. Mezirow, and E. W. Taylor (Eds.), *Transformative learning in practice: Insights from community, 39 workplace, and higher education* (pp. 18-32). Jossey Bass.

Mezirow, J. (2012). Learning to think like an adult: Core concepts of transformation theory. In E. Taylor, & P. Cranton (Eds.), *The handbook of transformative learning: Theory, research and practice* (pp. 73-96). Jossey-Bass.

Mezirow, J., & Associates. (2000). *The handbook of transformative learning: theory: Research and practice.* Jossey-Bass.

Michelson, E. (1998). Re-membering: The return of the body to experiential learning. *Studies in Continuing Education, 2*(1), 217-233.

Ng, R. (2005). Embodied pedagogy as transformative learning: A critical reflection. In S. Mojab & H. Nosheen (Eds.), *Proceedings of the Canadian Association for the Study of Adult Education (CASAE) 24th Annual Conference* (Vol. Canadian Association for the Study of Adult Education, pp. 155-161).

Pearson, C. M., Andersson, L. M., & Wegner, M. J. (2001). When workers flout convention: A study of workplace incivility. *Human Relations*, *54*(11), 1387-1419.

Perry, E. L., Kulik, C. T., & Schmidtke, J. M. (1998). Individual differences in the effectiveness of sexual harassment awareness training. *Journal of Applied Social Psychology*, *28*, 698-723.

Perry, E. L., Kulik, C. T., Golom, F. D., & Cruz, M. (2019). Sexual harassment training: Often necessary but rarely sufficient. *Industrial and Organizational Psychology*, *12*, 89-92.

Perry, E. L., Kulik, C. T., Bustamante, J., & Golom, F. D. (2010). The impact of reason for training on the relationship between 'best practices' and sexual harassment training effectiveness. *Human Resource Development Quarterly*, *21*(2), 187-208.

Perry, E. L., Kulik, C. T., & Bustamante, J. (2012). Factors impacting the knowing-doing gap in sexual harassment training. *Human Resource Development International*, *15*, 589-608.

Piercy, G. (2013). Transformative learning theory and spirituality: A whole person approach. *Journal of Instructional Research*, *2*, 30-42.

Porath, C., & Pearson, C. (2010). The cost of bad behaviour. *Organizational Dynamics*, *39*(1), 64-71.

Porath, C. & Pearson, C. (2013). The price of incivility: Lack of respect hurts morale—and the bottom line. *Harvard Business Review*, *91*(12), 114-121.

Quick, J. C., & McFadyen, M. A. (2017). Sexual harassment: Have we made any progress? *Journal of Occupational Health Psychology*, *22*(3), 286-298.

Rawski, S., Djurdjevic, E., Foster, J., & Soderberg, A. (2020). The role of trainer characteristics in intern sexual harassment training effectiveness. *Academy of Management Proceedings*. https://journals.aom.org/doi/pdf/10.5465/AMBPP.2020.78

Richman, J. A. (2004). The factor structure of generalized workplace harassment. *Violence and Victims*, *19*, 221-239.

Roehling, M. V., & Huang, J. (2018). Sexual harassment training effectiveness: An interdisciplinary review and call for research. *Journal of Organizational Behavior*, *39*, 134-150.

Bibliography

Salin, D. (2008). Organisational responses to workplace harassment: An exploratory study. *Personnel Review, 38*(1), 26-44.

Scerti, R. (2019, January 28). *Essential facilitation skills for an effective facilitation.* Session Lab. https://www.sessionlab.com/blog/facilitation-skills/

Schon, D. (1987). *Educating the reflective practitioner.* Jossey-Bass.

Shor, I., & Freire, P. (1987). What is the "Dialogical Method" of teaching? *Journal of Education, 169*(3), 11-31.

Singleton, J. (2015). *Head, heart, and hands model for transformative learning: Place as context for changing sustainability values.* http://www.jsedimensions.org/wordpress/wp- content/uploads/2015/03/PDF-Singleton-JSE-March-2015-Love-Issue.pdf

Sipos, Y., Battisti, B., & Grimm, K. (2008). Achieving transformative sustainability learning: Engaging head, hands and heart. *International Journal of Sustainability in Higher Education, 9*(1), 68-86.

Smith, B. (2018). *What it really takes to stop sexual harassment: Psychologists call for a comprehensive approach with real-world impact.* https://www.apa.org/monitor/2018/02/sexual-harassment

Smith, J. H. (2017). *Embodiment.* Oxford University Press.

Statistics Canada (2018). *Insights on Canadian society: Harassment in Canadian workplaces.* https://www150.statcan.gc.ca/n1/pub/75-006-x/2018001/article/54982-eng.htm

Taylor, E. W. (1998). The theory and practice of transformative learning: A critical review. (ERIC Monograph Information Series No. 374). *ERIC Clearinghouse on Adult, Career, and Vocational Education.*

Taylor, E. W. (2006). *A critical review of the empirical research of transformative learning (1999-2005)* [Paper presentation]. Adult Education Research Conference.

Taylor, E. W. (2007). An update of transformative learning theory: A critical review of the empirical research (1999-2005). *International Journal of Lifelong Education, 26,* 173-191.

Taylor, E. W., & Cranton, P. (2013). A theory in progress? Issues in transformative learning theory. *European Journal for Research on the Education and Learning of Adults, 4*(1), 33-47.

Taylor, E. W., & Cranton, P. (2012). *The handbook of transformative learning: Theory, research, and practice.* Jossey-Bass.

Taylor, F. W. (1947). *The principles of scientific management. Scientific management: Comprising shop management. The principles of scientific management and testimony before the special House committee.* Harper.

Tepper, J. R., & White, G. C. (2011). *Workplace harassment in academic environment.* https://scholarship.law.slu.edu/lj/vol56/iss1/5

The Angus Reid Institute. (2018). *#MeToo: Moment or movement?* https://angusreid.org/me-too/

The Canada Safety Council. (2019). *Working with the bully.* https://canadasafetycouncil.org/working-bully/

Tippett, E. C. (2018). *Harassment training. A content analysis.* https://ssrn.com/abstract=2994571

Tisdell, E. J. (2003). *Exploring spirituality and culture in adult and higher education.* Jossey-Bass.

Tisdell, E. J., & Tolliver, D. E. (2001). The role of spirituality in culturally relevant and transformative adult education. *Adult Learning, 12*(3), 13-14.

Van Loo, J. B., & Rocco, T. S. (2004). Continuing professional education and human capital theory. In *Academy of Human Resource Development International Conference*, 98-105.

Walsh, M. (2020). *Embodiment: Moving beyond mindfulness.* Unicorn Slayer Press.

Walsh, B. M., Bauerle, T. J., & Magley, V. J. (2013). Individual and contextual inhibitors of sexual harassment training motivation. *Human Resource Development Quarterly, 24*(2), 215-237.

Wellington, E. (2017, October 23). *Tarana Burke: MeToo Movement can't end with a hashtag.* https://www.philly.com/philly/columnists/elizabeth_wellington/philly-me-too-movement-founder-tarana-burke-20171023.html

York, K. M., Barclay, L. A., & Zajack, A. B. (1997). Preventing sexual harassment: The effect of multiple training methods. *Employee Responsibilities and Rights Journal, 10*(4), 277-289.

ABOUT THE AUTHOR

Dr. Candy Khan has over 25 years of experience embedding diversity, equity, and belonging principles into policies, programs, and services. Her extensive experience working with large organizations in the private, academic, not-for-profit, and public sectors includes both in-house consulting and leadership experience. Candy possesses a Doctorate in Education in the field of Adult Education in the Workplace from the University of Alberta, and a Master's in education in Theoretical, Cultural, and International Studies. She has a Bachelor of Arts in Psychology. Dr. Khan has deep experience developing curriculum and overseeing training programs across organizations with a range of training needs. She is also a qualified administrator for Intercultural Development Inventory, a certified change management expert, and a leadership coach, and has conducted many workplace investigations with a special focus on workplace restoration.

COMING SOON

*Working Wounded: Six Ways
to Manage Workplace Challenges*

*Employees' Perceptions of Anti-Harassment
Training Program Design:
Whole Person Pedagogical Approach*

*Love Letters to Zahra:
A memoir to my Grand Daughter*
(2023)

*How Not to Do a Doctorate:
A Personal Journey*
(2024)

www.ingramcontent.com/pod-product-compliance
Lightning Source LLC
Chambersburg PA
CBHW050255120526
44590CB00016B/2365